Bodo J. Baginski   **Shalila Sharamon**

REIKI
Universal Life Energy

Dear Nadia,
you touched my soul and
life in so many ways with
all your Gifts and Talents.
May you continue to make
a difference in the lives of
others and may your healing Hands
bring peace to Body, Mind and
Spirit.   Love, light and healing
yours alway Nadia

Dedicated

to all those involved

in the birth of a new age

UNIVERSAL LIFE ENERGY

**A Holistic Method of Treatment
for
the Professional Practice
Absentee Healing
and
Self-treatment
of Mind, Body and Soul**

Bodo J. Baginski   LIFERHYTHM   Shalila Sharamon

With 38 illustrations by Alois Hanslian and motifs by Bodo J. Baginski
Cover design: Shalila Sharamon
Graphic design: Bodo J. Baginski
Photo on page 27 by Vera Graham, The Times.

Translated into English by Christopher Baker and Judith Harrison

Library of Congress Cataloging-in Publication Data

Baginski, Bodo J.
  Reiki : universal life energy.
  Translated from the German.
  Bibliography:
  1. Mental healing.   I Sharamon, Shalila. II Title.
  RZ401.B1313 1988   615.8'51   88-13955
  ISBN 0-940795-02-7

First published in Germany as "Reiki—Universale Lebensenergie"
Copyright © Synthesis Verlag 1985
PO Box 14 32 06
45262 Essen, Germany

First printed in English 1988

Copyright © LifeRhythm 1988
PO Box 806
Mendocino CA 95460
Tel: (707) 937-1825 Fax: (707) 937-3052

Printed in the United States of America

Table of Contents

Please note: Reiki is Japanese and is pronounced "Ray-Key"

Introduction

When you read this book, your spirit will come into contact with ours. We will be sharing a special kind of knowledge with you, a knowledge that has proved to be so rich and valuable in itself that it seems as if this book came about without our doing.

If this is your first encounter with Reiki, it is our hope that it will mean the beginning of an acquaintance with one of the highest forms of energy in existence, and that a totally new dimension of life will be revealed to both you and those you know in the process.

Reiki isn't difficult to "learn" — indeed, it is the simplest healing method we know of. Special medical knowledge isn't necessary either, for the universal life energy of Reiki possesses a wisdom of its own and functions of its own accord.

If such a thought seems strange to you at first, then just think of the wisdom with which our bodies function, and how life develops and is sustained everywhere in creation independent of whether we know about it or not.

A sensation of inner bliss and harmony, which begins to *flow* during treatment, always accompanies *working* with this universal power. Afterwards, there is usually a feeling of just having experienced something especially beautiful. In contrast to what we are used to experiencing after other forms of treatment (which often prove to be tiring), we are filled with a sensation of peace, vitality and joy. It would seem that the healing and harmonizing effects of Reiki involve not only the patient but also the practitioner himself.

Reiki isn't a new invention or fad. Its origins have their roots in an old tradition that has been handed down over the centuries. Today we can use it to complement all other kinds of healing methods. Reiki is also a natural system of great simplicity, since nothing other than your hands are required to carry it out. At the same time, immediate relief can also be attained for all kinds of complaints. For these reasons we believe that it will be established as a recognized form of natural healing one day.

We frequently use the term "patient" in this book, but this does not mean to say that we only treat people who are ill in the usual sense of the word. Our patients are often people simply in search of harmony and relaxation while others are seeking an increased sense of vitality or help for their spiritual paths. The word "patient" is derived from *"patentia,"* which is Latin for patience. In other words, a patient is a person who has to be patient about something. This something does not always have to be an illness, it can concern anything that we experience as a restriction or barrier on our life's journey. In this sense, everyone who receives Reiki is a patient, even though he may not need to be healed of any special ailment other than to be made *"whole"* (or *"healed"* in the broadest sense of the word).

In this respect, the term "practitioner" (or "therapist", as practitioners are often known in Germany) is also not to be understood in the usual sense. The word therapist for example is derived from *"therapeua,"* which is Greek for someone who "assists someone on his path." The original meaning of this word can well be applied to the passing on of Reiki, even when there is no specific illness or complaint.

Now we would like to invite you to accompany us through this book, where we will try to acquaint you with Reiki.

In case you are already familiar with the Usui system of Reiki, we hope you will find new ideas and tips in our book to confirm and increase your experience of Reiki.

It was our goal to write a book which would not only appeal to the interested layman but also to the professional in his practice. For ourselves, writing this book has not only given us much pleasure but also proved to be source of inspiration.

At this point, we would like to express our gratitude to Brigitte Müller, our Reiki Master, who conveyed to us her knowledge of Reiki in a very loving manner. Further thanks are also due to all the other people who supported our work on this book, especially Alois Hanslian, a friend of ours who has complemented and enriched the text with his beautiful and expressive illustrations.

We wish you much joy in the reading of this book and love, harmony and growth on your inner path.

About the Authors

It has always interested us to know what the person hidden behind the written words of a book is actually like. We have always wanted to know which pathway he has taken and how his life manifests his knowledge. Usually the reader is only told a few selected facts about an author, and the distance generally remains great. Therefore, we would like to tell you a few things about ourselves so that you can form an idea of the people sharing their knowledge and experience of Reiki with you.

Shalila, by Bodo

I was staying at a nice little meditation academy when a very delicate-looking girl with long blonde hair sat down and exchanged a few words with me. The next day I met her again in the academy greenhouse where I learned in passing that this blonde "girl" was acually 36 years old and that she had founded and led the academy herself for a long time. Shortly after this, I saw her making some very reasonable furniture with the simplest of tools. Shalila was beginning to really confuse me.

A few months later she told me about the path she had taken through life. As a child, she had often felt as if she were a stranger to this world. There were so many things which could not be explained, and when spiritual experiences started happening to her at an early age, she felt very alone, sometimes thinking she was simply not meant for this world.

About 14 years ago, this state of affairs underwent a complete change when she started meditating and met an Indian guru. For the first time in her life she found an answer to her questions and an explanation for her "strange" experiences. It did not take long before she was being trained to teach meditation herself, something which was to become her task in life, for she was soon giving numerous lectures, founding new meditation centres and guiding hundreds of people to meditation. Then began a series of long journeys which led her to the spiritual healers of the Philippines as well as to India, Thailand, Israel, Greece and other countries.

A few weeks after my move to the academy, Shalila told us that she wished to withdraw into the woods for a while. No one knew what she did during this time. She was living in a farmhouse near the academy and we saw her very seldom. One day she read me parts of a book she was planning which she had written in the peace of a secluded clearing. The text sounded like spiritual fairy-tales. I was both astonished and fascinated, for these were the subtlest and most profound words that I had ever heard. (The book in question is still not finished, but will be published one day.)

Shalila is more sensitive than I am, and her intuition is more pronounced, too. Today, she has a very loving relationship to her parents, who support her on her path with much understanding. For some time she has been carrying out astrological sittings (in holistic astrology) following years of preparation. These sittings are intended to draw people's attention to their real goals in life as well as to their tasks and gifts and to show them how these are to be realized. Every now and then she translates a book, normally dealing with spiritual matters. She has been practising the Sidhi technique for many years and deals with cheirology and dream work too.

The first time I gave Reiki to Shalila, she was absolutely delighted with the results. She felt wonderfully protected and pervaded by a feeling of light, and many emotions were set free. She developed the desire to pass on Reiki herself, which she was soon able to do. Shalila found "working" with Reiki much easier than I had at the beginning since she wasn't encumbered with medical knowledge to the extent that I was. In the meantime, we carry out Reiki treatments together.

Shalila's outer style of life is very simple. Since she travels a lot and works at different places, she has reduced her possessions to a carefully chosen minimum. Her few clothes she sews herself, and she eats almost only grain sprouts, fruit and salads. I seldom hear her say a negative word, for she spontaneously sees the positive side to things first. Her dealings with the world are based on trust, and the love and support she receives in return have proved her right in this respect.

I am very glad to be able to work with Shalila. She says that Reiki has enriched her life to a great extent, has greatly increased the depth of her meditation and has brought her much inner happiness and satisfaction.

Bodo, by Shalila

When I returned to our small meditation academy after a long journey, I found myself looking into a pair of unknown blue eyes which regarded the world both lovingly and peacefully. It was with pleasure that I heard that they belonged to Bodo, a new member of the academy administration. It soon turned out that Bodo was a blessing for our community. There was no area of work where he did not enjoy helping out, whether organizing courses, washing dishes, repairing the  swimming-pool's circulatory system, taking care of the greenhouse, or preparing delicious meals. Bodo never tired of doing what he could, and the talent he displayed in the process was impressive.

Bodo had been living a few weeks in our academy when I came across two of his books — one with wonderfully moving poems and the other a lively collection of well-observed short stories. The authors of both these books were his parents, Bodo and Olli Baginski.

A little while later I was to get to know these authors personally. Never in my life have I been given such a welcome as was the case during this visit to the home of Bodo's parents. I began to wonder what the childhood of the boy had been like who had grown up in such harmonious surroundings. The answer I got was that it had been "very rebellious". It was school that Bodo had above all been unable to accept. Something in him refused to learn so many "useless" things, and at times he would run home during break, pack a rucksack and set off on journeys throughout various European countries without a penny to his name. Impatience and an urge for independence drove him away from his school books more than once.

At the age of 12, he began going to a Steiner school, and finally began to develop a taste for learning. There now followed a time of searching, where music, painting and treating people crystallized as his main talents. In 1970, he underwent training to become a physiotherapist, grasping his studies quickly and easily. His dynamic character and sense of responsibility soon led to his becoming entrusted with leading posts, and it was soon after this that he opened his first practice. He made his home on the East Fresian islands, off the northern coast of West Germany. Here the breadth of the sea, its peacefullness and solitude have drawn him back time and time again and reflect a further facet of his many-sided personality.

Even in those days he developed an interest for alternative healing methods and began undergoing training in those areas. A further talent of Bodo's also made itself felt during this time — his interest for technical advances in this area of medicine, which led him to develop his own apparatus and equipment. Within two years, he opened a larger practice which possessed every kind of equipment necessary for physiotherapy.

At the age of 27 he had everything he ever wanted — his own business, a nice home and a high income — yet, at the same time, he felt it wasn't all there was to life. He became more and more conscious of the fact that most of his methods of treatment only dealt with the outer symptoms of disturbances and that they neglected the patient in his totality of body, mind and soul.

Having carried out his profession for ten years, Bodo burnt his bridges behind him and sold his house and practice to open himself to new perspectives. His path led him to Findhorn, the well-known spiritual community in North Scotland, where he spent the summer carrying out his favorite hobby, painting pictures which revealed his inner world, using colors he made himself.

When he later told me about this, he showed me some photographs of what he had painted. I found myself lost in wonderful expanses of light and color, lent space and structure by crystal shapes and pyramidical forms.

It was in Findhorn that he began learning various alternative methods of healing and he has continued to grow in the years since. At the moment, he not only possesses knowledge of all the conservative methods of treatment used in physiotherapy but has also undergone training in Hand and Foot Refloxotherapy, Prenatal Therapy (Metamorphic Method), Touch For Health (Applied Kinesiology), Polarity, Meridian Therapy, Balneotherapy, Acidosis Therapy, Spiritual Healing, Psychocybernetics, Superlearning methods, dream work, fasting and natural nutrition. In all these methods he has had many years of experience.

Each new method of treatment brought him valuable ideas and experience. Yet he always had the feeling that there had to be something more holistic, something that would be more direct and more all-embracing in effect. This feeling was confirmed the first time he came into contact with Reiki.

Today, Bodo treats almost only with Reiki, and this has been justified by the results. His lectures on Reiki and other alternative healing methods, which he delivers with much warmth and sincerity while displaying a wealth of qualified knowledge, have led many people to a deeper understanding of life and helped them to set new perspectives for themselves.

I am very happy to be able to work with Bodo. I am grateful that he led me to Reiki.

Purpose

*Expansion of happiness
is the purpose of creation
and we are all here
to enjoy and radiate
happiness everywhere.*

Maharishi Mahesh Yogi

CHAPTER 1
What is Reiki?

"Reiki is wisdom and truth"
Hawayo Takata

Throughout the history of mankind healing methods have always existed which were based on the transfere of a universal, all-pervading life energy, the same energy which brings forth all life in the universe and nourishes it. Thousands of years ago the Tibetans already possessed a deep understanding of the nature of spirit, energy and matter, using this knowledge to heal their bodies, harmonize their souls and lead their spirits to an experience of unity. We come across this knowledge later again in India and find modified forms of it in the Japanese, Chinese, Egyptian, Greek and Roman cultures, just to mention a few.

This knowledge was guarded and preserved by the mystery schools of most ancient cultures and was available in its entirety only to very few people, usually priests or spiritual leaders who in turn passed it on to their disciples by word of mouth.

Modern scholars often come across handed-down forms of this *inner knowledge* but generally misinterpret it because it is usually shrouded in cryptic language and symbols. The knowledge of Reiki would have remained lost forever had not Dr. Mikao Usui rediscovered the key which led to the recovery of a thousand-year old tradition of healing in 2,500-year-old Sanskrit sutras at the end of the 19th century.

The word Reiki means universal life energy. It is defined as being that power which acts and lives in all created matter. The word consists of two parts. The syllable *rei* describes the universal, boundless aspect of this energy while *ki* is in itself part of *rei,* being the vital life force energy which flows through all living beings.

Many races, cultures and religions have always been aware of the existence of an energy which corresponds to the meaning of *ki.* Thus ki is named:

Chi by the Chinese,
ight, or *Holy Ghost* by Christians,
Prana by the Hindus,
Mana by the Kahunas and
Bioplasmic energy by Russians researchers

And it is conceivable and probable that
   the *Telesma* of Hermes Trismegistos,
   the *Ka* of the Egyptians,
   the *Pneuma* of the Greeks,
   the *Eckankar* of the Pali language,
   the *Baraka* of the Sufis,
   the *Fluid of Life* of the Alchemists,
   the *Jesod* of the Jewish Cabbalists,
   the *Mgebe* of the Huri pygmies,
   the *Elima* of the Nikundo,
   the *Hasina* on the island of Madagascar,
   the *Wakan* or *Wakouda* of the Sioux,
   the *Oki* of Hurone Indians,
   the power of European kings to touch by healing,
   the *Orende* of the Irokese,
   the *lan vital* of Henri Bergson,
   the *Numia* of Paracelcus,
   the *Healing Power of Nature* of Hippocrates,
   the *Orgon* of Dr. Wilhelm Reich,
   the *Odic Power* of Baron Reichenbach,
   the *Universal Life Power* of Baron Ferson,
   the *Tellurism* of Prof. G. Kieser,
   the *Biocosmic Energy* of Dr. O. Brunler,
   the *X Power* of L. E. Eemann and
   the *Fifth Power*

are all one and the same basic energy, although the extent to which they are
applied and the theories concerning them differ greatly. The basic conditions required for making use of this energy are also very different. Some of
the systems named require that long drawn-out exercises be carried out
beforehand and frequently much privation must be endured before the
desired energy can be drawn upon and made use of.
The closer we approach the basic form of this universal energy of life, the

more comprehensive and effective it will become and the easier it will be to use. As a piece of hermetic wisdom says:

"The seal of truth is simplicity."

The Usui system of Reiki is not only the most simple and natural healing method we know of, but it is also the most effective way of transferring this universal life energy. Once a person has been opened up to become a "channel" for Reiki, concentrated life energy will flow through his hands of its own accord and he will retain this ability for the rest of his life. What exactly *is* this universal life energy. Let us first hear what both wise men of old and the scientists of today have to say on the subject.

It is owing to modern-day physics that most people on earth today are aware of the tremendous "vitality" which pervades all existence. It wasn't so long ago after all that that a stone was thought of as being "dead" matter. Today we now know that such "simple" things consist of an intricate and intelligent interrelationship of innumerable forces. How small is such a stone compared to the enormous expanse of our universe. How simple is it in construction compared to the human body, which consists of about 100 billion (100,000,000,000,000) cells. These cells in turn possess about 100,000 differing genes, consisting of long, spiral-formed DNA chains. Every single one of these microscopically small cells contains within itself no less than the total genetic construction plans for our bodies.

If we were to roll out all these spiralled chains and join them up, their length would amount to more than 120 billion kilometres, about 800 times the distance between the earth and the sun. And yet all these chains of DNA molecules fit into the size of a walnut!

The game with figures and values could be carried on without end. How immeasurably great then must be the energy that all these forms of life manifest. How immeasurably great must be the intelligence which gives these forms of life shape and structure. Or did our universe and our lives arise out of a chain of coincidences, as a materialistic view of things would have us believe? Can unconscious matter bring forth consciousness? Can it bring about spirit? Can it bring about a soul? At this point even science is faced with an unsolved problem. Many scientists reached the point in their work where there is only one explanation left, namely that a superior intelligent force *does* exist: a *universal* spirit which is continually creating the universe out of itself.

The latest developments in quantum physics come very close to this idea. Supergravitation theory describes the existence of a standardized, perfectly balanced field standing in relationship to only itself, *a field of pure intelligence* which brings forth all matter to form the basis of all creation. This coincides exactly with the statements which wise and enlightened men have been making throughout the centuries. They tell us that there is a state of being which contains all creation and out of which all life arose. The energy of this state of being lives in all things, and it is this universal energy which flows through our hands in concentrated form when we treat someone with Reiki.

The meaning of this in practical terms is that Reiki is above all holistic in effect. It reaches all levels of existence and strives to bring these differing levels into a state of balance. The therapist is only a channel for this energy, for it is not his own, limited energy which passes through him when he lays his hands on a person, but rather a universal one, which leaves him strengthened and harmonized afterwards. Reiki also makes its own way to the area of the body in need of treatment. It is obviously endowed with a greater wisdom than our own, for it seems to know where and how and to what extent a patient needs it without our being able to add to or subtract from the effect it produces.

Very receptive people often experience Reiki as love. Love is a uniting power which leads us forward to an even greater state of oneness with the whole of creation. The real goal of mankind is to translate this state into reality and to live it out. Love is the original home of the soul, where it returns to be united as a drop with the boundless ocean of being, a state of union encompassing knowledge and wisdom, creativity and harmony as well as self-realization, all-embracing love and eternal bliss.

Reiki can help us to find our way back to this state of health or wholeness (holiness). It is a healing method in the broadest sense of the word.

As you will have already noticed, Reiki has nothing to do with spiritualism or the occult in any shape or form. It has nothing to do with the calling up of ghosts or demons, nor is it concerned with hypnosis or any other kind of psychological technique. Giving Reiki won't make you a "magician" or "psycho-conjuror." In Reiki treatment, use is made solely of a neutral but concentrated from of cosmic energy.

To practise Reiki, no special kind of faith or belief is required. It is used with the same successs by people of many faiths and religions, by free thinkers as well as by the followers of widely differing philosophies and ideologies. The fact that Reiki has enabled many people to arrive at a more comprehensive understanding of religious matters while enabling them to experience spirituality in a more profound manner speaks for its universality.

It is surely no coincidence that a method of healing like Reiki has been rediscovered and brought back to life in our day and age, for recognition of the fact that the deeper wisdoms of life form a counterpart to the one-sided development of science and technology has brought about a new concern with just these very truths.

We are standing on the threshold of a *new age* which will either be brought about by a new quality of human consciousness or else by the radical destruction of old, outlived structures. Whatever happens, it is our decision and we find it encouraging to observe how interest in the Truth is spreading. We are in agreement with Robert Jungk when he says:

"Mankind is not yet done with.
Challenged by deadly dangers
he is spurred to unfold himself and develop."

The only thing that can unfold within us are those abilities which were always there, folded away and waiting to be developed. The Reiki art of healing is one of these wonderful abilities.

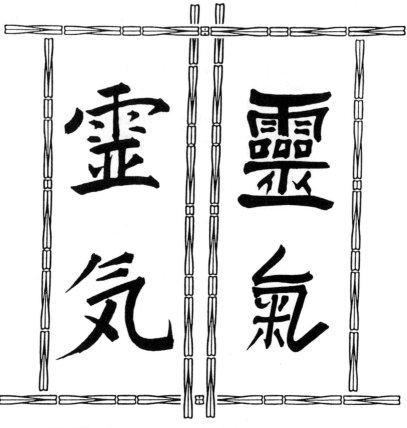

"Reiki" written in Japanese in different styles of writing

"Reiki" written in a manner frequently used by the Reiki Alliance

CHAPTER 2
The History of Reiki

The ancient healing method of Reiki was re-discovered in the middle of the nineteenth century by Dr. Mikao Usui, who was also responsible for its revival. The story of Dr. Usui's search for this secret knowledge has been told by Grand Master Hawayo Takata (1900-1980) along the following lines: Mikao Usui was the principal of a Christian seminary in Kyoto, Japan. One day, some of his older pupils asked him why they had heard nothing of the healing methods used by Jesus Christ and whether Dr. Usui would be able to carry out such a healing for them. Since he was unable to answer these questions, Dr. Usui decided to give up his position and study Christianity in a Christian country until he had found the answers.

His journey led him to America, where he attended the University of Chicago and became a Doctor of Theology. However, he could not find a satisfactory answer in Christian writings and, not having found one in Chinese scripts either, he travelled to North India, where he was able to study the Holy Writings. Dr. Usui had not only command of Japanese, Chinese and English but also of Sanskrit.

He later returned to Japan, where he discovered some Sanskrit formulas and symbols in old Bhuddist sutras which seemed to hold the answers to his questions. At the time, he was living in a monastery in Kyoto and, after he had spoken to the Head, he set off to the Holy Mountain of Kuriyama, which lay 16 miles away. Here he intended to fast and meditate in solitude for 21 days in the hope of gaining contact with the level of consciousness the Sanskrit symbols had been written on in order to determine the truth of their contents.

On his arrival at the mountain, he placed 21 little stones in front of him and removed one at the passing of each day as a kind of calendar. During this time, he read in the Sutras, sang and meditated. Nothing unusual happened until the last day dawned. It was still quite dark when he saw a shining light moving towards him with great speed. It became bigger and bigger and finally hit him in the middle of the forehead. Dr. Usui thought he was going to die when he suddenly saw millions of little bubbles in blue, lilac, pink

Dr. Mikao Usui

and all the colors of the rainbow. A great white light appeared, and he saw the well-known Sanskrit symbols in front of him glowing in shining gold and he said, "Yes, I remember."

Thus was the birth of the Usui system of Reiki.

When he returned to a normal state of consciousness, the sun was standing high in the sky. He felt full of strength and energy and began to climb down the mountain. In his rush, however, he stubbed his toe. He held it with his hands for a few minutes and the bleeding stopped and the pain disappeared. This was the first miracle.

Since he was hungry, he stopped at an inn at the wayside and ordered a large Japanese breakfast. The innkeeper warned him not to eat such a large meal after fasting so long, but Dr. Usui was able to eat it all without the least of consequences. This was the second miracle.

The granddaughter of the innkeeper had a bad toothache, from which she had been suffering for several days. Dr. Usui laid his hands on her swollen face and she immediately felt better. She ran to her grandfather and told him that their guest was no ordinary monk. This healing was the third miracle of the day.

Dr. Usui returned to his monastery but decided after a few days to go to Beggar City in the slums of Kyoto to treat the beggars and help them lead a better life. He spent seven years in the asylum, treating many illnesses.

One day, however, he noticed that the same old faces kept returning. When he asked why they had not begun a new life he was told that working was too troublesome and that it was better to go on begging.

Dr. Usui was deeply shaken and wept. He recognized that he had forgotten something of great importance in his healing, namely to teach the beggars gratitude. In the following days he thought out some Reiki maxims which are to be found at the end of the chapter.

Soon afterwards he left the asylum and returned to Kyoto, where he kindled a large torch and stood in the streets. Asked the reason why by passers-by, he told them he was looking for people in search of the true Light, people who were ill and oppressed and who were longing to be healed. This was the beginning of a new part of his life, which he spent travelling around and teaching Reiki.

Dr. Usui is now buried in a Kyoto temple, with the story of his life written on his gravestone. It is said that his grave was honored by the Emperor of Japan.

One of Dr. Usui's closest collaborators, Dr. Chijiro Hayashi, took his place, becoming the second Reiki Grand Master in the line of tradition. He ran a private Reiki clinic in Tokyo until 1940, where unusally severe cases could be

Dr. Chijiro Hayashi
Died 1941

Grand Master Hawayo Takata
1900-1980

treated, with Reiki being applied "round-the-clock" in the event of especially serious illnesses. Frequently a patient would also receive Reiki from several practitioners at once. The effects of the Second World War and the death of Dr. Hayashi on May 10, 1941, put an end to this work. Hawaya Takata became Dr. Hayashi's successor. She was born in 1900 on the island of Hawaii as the child of Japanese parents but was a citizen of the United States. She was a widow with two small children and at the end of her physical and spiritual strength when her path led her to Reiki in 1935. She was suffering from a number of severe illnesses at the time when an inner voice told her to go to Japan and seek healing there.

Having arrived in Japan, she was lying on the operating table, about to undergo an operation, when the voice spoke to her again, telling her that the operation was unnecessary. She asked her doctor about other methods of treatment and he advised her to go to Dr. Hayashi's Reiki clinic. Once there, she was applied Reiki daily by two practitioners and, after a few months, she had won back her health completely.

Hawayo Takata became a pupil of Dr. Hayashi's for a year and then returned to Hawaii with her daughters. She was made a Reiki Master by Dr. Hayashi when he visited Hawaii in 1938. On his death in 1941, she succeeded him as Grand Master. She lived and healed in Hawaii for many years, but she first began to train Reiki masters herself when she was in her seventies. On 11, December, 1980, Hawayo Takata passed away, leaving 22 Reiki masters in the USA and Canada.

Shortly before her decease, Hawayo Takata and some of the Reiki masters grounded in August 1980 the **American Reiki Association** which was to organize and co-ordinate the passing on of the knowledge of Reiki.

Today, Reiki is represented by two organizations which have succeeded the first and which are both based in the USA. One has been **The American International Reiki Association, Inc.** (A.I.R.A., now called T.R.T.A.I.) and the other is **The Reiki Alliance.**

The Reiki Alliance was founded in 1981 by Phyllis Lee Furumoto, the granddaughter of the former Grand Master, and a group of 21 Reiki Masters, in the form of an open association. The "Reiki Alliance" was registered in the USA as a non-profit organization in 1981, with Phyllis Lee Furumoto holding the position of Grand Master. At the beginning of 1987, about 100 Reiki Masters, some of them living in Europe, were members of the Alliance. Most of the Masters trained by Hawayo Takata belong to this organization. The Reiki Alliance takes a spiritual approach to the spreading of Reiki and keeps to the traditional teachings. The Alliance is of the opinion that the

Hawayo Takata in 1975

Truth finds its way to the hearts of those open and prepared for it and, therefore, they rarely advertise.

The **American International Reiki Association Inc. (A.I.R.A)** was founded-ed in 1982, by Dr. Barbara Weber Ray. Dr. Ray had also been trained by Hawaya Takata to convey the knowledge involved in the attainment of the Master grade to others and became the President of this group. The A.I.R.A. has been concerned with research into scientific aspects of Reiki to a large extent and is known for its well organized publicity efforts. It has founded a Reiki documentation center and carries out symposiums, conferences and exhibitions and is active in public events. The Association also trains teachers of Reiki.

We are of the opinion that both organizations complement each other in their efforts to teach and spread the idea of Reiki. If you wish to join one of them, search your heart, rely on your intuition and join the organization that best answers your needs. We have worked with Reiki practitioners from both groups and the experience was positive in every case.

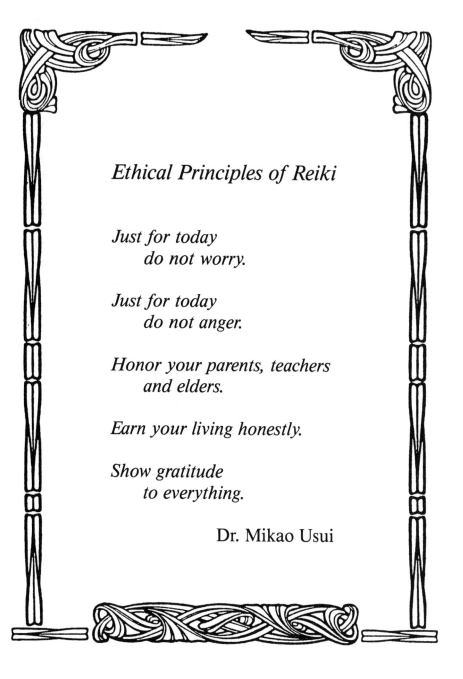

Ethical Principles of Reiki

*Just for today
    do not worry.*

*Just for today
    do not anger.*

*Honor your parents, teachers
    and elders.*

Earn your living honestly.

*Show gratitude
    to everything.*

Dr. Mikao Usui

CHAPTER 3
How Does Reiki Work?

"Reiki — the greatest secret in the science of energetics"
Hawayo Takata

You probably want to know how Reiki works and what it feels like to both practitioner and patient. In this respect, we would first of all like to quote some Reiki recipients.

Following her first treatment, an old lady of 80 years recounted, "I have never experienced such a deep sense of relaxation in all my life. I was filled with a feeling of peace and quiet and everything inside me was very spacious. I felt how it began to work on the ill parts of my body and I am amazed that there is something as wonderful as Reiki."

An elderly gentleman reports, "It was quite different today. My legs prickled all the time and I was very restless."

A young girl said, "It was nice and relaxing but nothing special happened. Is it meant to be that way?"

A woman teacher says "I saw so many things — images, colors and wonderful landscapes. It was quite something!"

These few examples are meant to demonstrate that each person reacts in a different way to Reiki. Since it works where the recipient needs it most, no general rule can be said to exist. The most common thing experienced during treatment is a sense of peace and relaxation, often combined with a pleasant feeling of security and of being enclosed in a fine sheathe of energy. But even this won't be experienced every time. What can be stated with finality, however, is the fact that Reiki works holistically.

When we treat someone with Reiki, we do this by laying our hands gently on the various parts of the body with our fingers closed tight.* We will soon feel a kind of flowing sensation, often combined with a sensation of warmth, which can turn into heat or become quite cold. The patient will often feel the flowing as noticeably as we do, as well as the sensation of hot

---

* Please compare with the Bible, Mark 16.18

and cold. On some occasions, he will also sense warmth at a different part of the body than where we feel it, or what he experiences as warmth is cold for us.

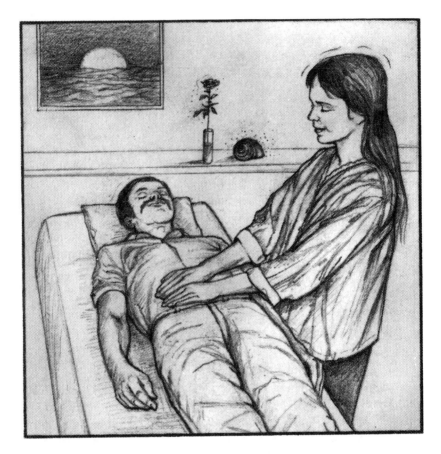

It is interesting to note that a thermometer placed between the practitioner's hands and the patient's body will not register a noticeable change in temperature. Obviously, the change that is experienced as taking place cannot be measured physically.

Most Reiki recipients begin to relax during treatment and may even fall asleep, but this won't make any difference in the effects of treatment. On other occasions, old and unresolved experiences may become conscious again. A release of emotions can occur and tears will flow or a laugh of relief will be released. It has also been known for experiences of a strongly visual character to occur; this may take on a visionary character in the case of people who regularly practise a form of meditation. It can also occur that a series of treatment will bring about dissolution of inner barriers which had been blocking holistic growth.

Although we lay our hands on the patient's body in order to link him to the energy of Reiki, it won't merely affect him on the material plane but will involve him in his entirety of mind, body and spirit.

Bodily illness or weakness is only the physical expression of a lack of basic order, a sign of having fallen out of a state of inner union with all life. In this respect, we would like to quote Dr. Edward Bach (1886-1936), the founder of a system of healing using flower remedies which is now named after him. As Dr. Bach* says:

> *"Disease will never be cured or eradicated by present materialistic methods, for the simple reason that disease in its origin is not material. What we know as disease is . . . the end product of deep and long acting forces."*

We can see that Reiki will bring us a decisive step closer to an original state of order. Reiki energy cannot be explained along our usual lines of therapeutic thinking. When someone is treated with Reiki, he is brought back into a state of unity with the harmony of the universe. This harmony, which is able to reach him in his smallest of cells, makes him whole and healthy again, thus encouraging the natural ability of the patient to heal himself.

Reiki leads us back to a state of wholeness in the widest sense of the word. It frequently happens that patients will come into contact with new ideas after a few Reiki treatments. Some will start doing yoga or autogenous training or start to meditate or practise some other kind of spiritual method. Others will read books on positive thinking, change their eating habits or even train to become Reiki practitioners themselves. Some patients will become aware of problems that had been repressed all along and find solutions for them. It is not seldom that a person will also find the courage to take certain new steps or develop the wish to change something in his life. It has always been our policy to encourage our patients to follow these positive impulses.

When you start working with Reiki you will notice that the effects of treatment may differ from what you had been expecting. We have made the

---

* "Heal Thyself," by Edward Bach, C.W. Daniel Co Ltd. London
  "The Twelve Healers and other Remedies," by Edward Bach, C.W. Daniel Co Ltd. London
  "The Bach Remedies Repertory," by Dr. Frances J. Wheeler, C.W. Daniel Co Ltd. London

observation again and again that Reiki has a "logic" of its own, knowing where and to what extent it is required. For this reason, it is not necessary to make a diagnosis before treatment, a fact that spares us no few mistakes. Every now and then patients come with certain complaints only to discover after treatment that other things have been helped, things which were apparently of top priority in the holistic order of healing. For example, once a woman came to us on the recommendation of a friend for treatment of complaints in the shoulder and lower neck region. Her friend had been helped by Reiki immediately, and the new patient was expecting something similar to happen. The second time she came she was rather disappointed because this had not been the case. In the course of the conversation that followed, she told us that on returning to her shop after the first treatment, the tense feeling she always had towards her customers had suddenly disappeared. This surprised her a great deal. She now felt light and relaxed and in a certain sense united with her customers. It became clear that her attitude towards her customers had always been sceptical and reserved and bound up with an inner fear of always having to defend herself. Now all these feelings were gone. She had even embraced a customer, a gesture she wouldn't normally have dreamed of. Weren't these the problems which were the cause of her complaints? How would her neck react when she no longer lived in a state of permanent tension?

She was an intelligent woman and, after a little talk, soon understood the interrelationship of psyche and body. From this point on the vicious circle of her complaints was broken, and she has since sent us many of her customers for treatment.

During a visit to the Philippines for a few months at the end of 1984, we treated many people who came to us out of the nearby jungle. One of the women was barren — probably one of the worst complaints a woman of 30 years of age can have on those islands. We treated her, and a few days later she told us that her digestion troubles, which she had been suffering for many years, had disappeared completely. Her stomach was now better, too, and when she was united in love with her husband she no longer felt any pain at all. These were all problems we knew nothing of beforehand. Without any conscious manipulation on our part, or the use of analytic thought, Reiki had once again made its way.

Symptoms can disappear completely without our having expected this to happen at all. For example, a patient once came to our practice with a complaint of the knees which he had had for decades. We saw little hope for him, for what changes could possibly occur after so many years? And yet, a few Reiki treatments freed him of his complaints for a very long time.

We will now list all the effects Reiki can have :

○ REIKI supports the body's natural ability to heal itself;
○ REIKI vitalizes both body and soul;
○ REIKI re-establishes spiritual equilibrium and mental well-being;
○ REIKI functions on all levels, whether mental or spiritual, bodily or emotional;
○ REIKI balances the body's energies;
○ REIKI loosens up blocked energy and promotes a state of total relaxation;
○ REIKI cleanses the body of poisons;
○ REIKI adjusts itself according to the needs of the recipient;
○ REIKI works with animals and plants; and
○ REIKI is an extremely pleasant, holistic method of healing.

We would like to add here that Reiki can never do damage in any way, since it only flows in the quantities necessary for the recipient.
What effect does Reiki have on the practitioner? What does he feel, what does he experience when he is treating someone with it? We have already mentioned that we are only a channel for Reiki. We are not the source of this energy; rather we place ourselves at its disposal as a kind of catalyst. No special kind of power or ability is necessary and no great effort is required. On the contrary, while we direct the flow of Reiki to a patient's body, we are being charged with it ourselves at the same time.
We frequently experience a sense of flowing in our hands. Bodo often has the feeling of sparks flying away from his hands, as if flashes of energy were jumping over to the patient. This is always a pleasant and harmonious experience for him. The experience Shalila has above all is a deep feeling of inner union with the patient. She often intuitively senses a patient's lacks while she is treating him. Afterwards we feel happy and physically and spiritually balanced.
A doctor, who once watched Bodo a few times while he was treating someone with Reiki, asked him afterwards if it weren't boring for him to simply lay his hands on a patient's body. Bodo told him, "Not at all. It always fascinates me to feel where and how the Reiki energy is flowing. I'm never bored when I'm doing it. On the contrary, I become more and more awake all the time." Today this doctor treats with Reiki himself.
What is also remarkable is the fact that more than 50 of our patients have asked us whether they could learn Reiki themselves, especially when compared to the fact that not even five of Bodo's former patients showed any

interest in learning the techniques applied to them in the fifteen years of his physiotherapeutic work.

We would also like to mention here that treatment with Reiki can result in the appearance of a slight or more vehement detoxication symptom on the physical level. These symptoms are to be regarded as a biologically sensible means of self-regulation. They generally take on the form of increased evacuation of the bowels and bladder, and increased mucus secretion in the upper respiratory passages, while a burning watering of the eyes can also occur. Sometimes the ears and skin will exude an increased amount of poisons and waste products. A short attack of fever or a temporary return of an earlier illness are also possible. These occurrences are to be regarded as a valuable means of recovering bodily health and not as a return of illness, representing as they do an absolutely natural cleansing mechanism. These reactions only last a short time, and the patient will generally feel all the better for them. They are similar to those symptoms which are known to occur after a long period of fasting,

"The best methods are those which help the life energy to resume its inner work of healing."

Paramahansa Yogananda*

It may be of interest to medical insiders to hear that Reiki therapy may cause previous illnesses to reappear and run a shortened course in accordance with a phenomenon first defined by the eminent physician and homeopath, Constantine Hering, and known in accordance as Hering's Law of Cure. In more modern times the same phenomenon has been described in greater detail by the German doctor Dr. med. H.H. Reckeweg. According to his terminology, Reiki treatment can induce a regressive vicariation from the so-called impregnation, degeneration and neoplasma phases towards the deposition, reaction and excretion phases. (On Reckeweg's "6-Phase Homotoxicosis Table"** this means a shift of the course of pathological development from the bottom right to the upper left.) Illnesses previously suffered are experienced briefly again in reverse order, signifying a genuine and natural cure, a phenomenon that may occur as a result of Reiki treatment.

* "Autobiography of a Yogi," by Paramahansa Yogananda, Self-Realization Fellowship, Los Angeles, 1946

** "Die Homotoxinlehre als Fundament der allgemeinen Pathologie und Therapie", Dr. med. H.H. Reckeweg, Aurelia Verlag, Baden-Baden, 1961, West Germany
"Die Homotoxikosen 6-Phasen-Tabelle", Dr. med. H.H. Reckeweg, Aurelia Verlag, Baden-Baden, West Germany

Dr. Reckeweg's discoveries were fundamental and well thought out, yet they were limited to the material level. The same mechanism which he observed and analyzed as taking place on the physical level occurs on mental and spiritual levels, too. Earlier, unresolved experiences and problems can be brought back to consciousness where they can be resolved and laid to one side as being "finished." In this manner, tensions, which are often rooted in the past and are the cause of blockages in the present, can be neutralized with the help of Reiki.

If you treat with Reiki to a great extent, similar reactions to the ones described above may happen to you, too. This is because when you treat someone with Reiki, it will be flowing through your hands and yourself, unfolding its healing power within you at the same time as the patient. Thus by passing Reiki on to others, you yourself will be cleansed more and more and made whole and healthy. You will notice that trust will slowly begin to develop within you, trust in a wisdom and power that will pervade your whole life. A new development will take place, leading you to insight and knowledge, to a conscious sense of unity with the whole of creation, and to love.

Receive
Just for the moment
set aside your conditioned
ideas and expectations
Make yourself empty for a moment.
Be open.
Receive.

CHAPTER 4
Is it Necessary to Believe in it?

Are you a sceptical sort of person? One objection we often hear during our lectures is that "All these methods only help when you believe in them. It is well-known that if you believe in something, anything will help."

Sometimes Bodo asks such critical people why they don't practise what they preach. All they need to do to get healthy again is believe in anything, whether doctor, tablet or religion. Why don't they do it then? Could it be that they don't believe in what they believe?

To really believe in something can without doubt be very helpful. But what is the case when someone is unconscious and only conscious belief in something will heal him? What about babies and small children? How can animals and plants be treated with success if this is true? What am I, the practitioner to do, if a patient tells me he doesn't believe in my method of treatment?

The fact that Reiki will help in all these cases has been confirmed thousands of times. "The American International Reiki Association" has founded a research institute where the steadily increasing amount of evidence proving the effectiveness of Reiki can be documented. Of course, it has not yet been possible to find satisfactory scientific explanations for all the phenomena occurring in respect to Reiki, nor for its successes and apparent failures, but there are many things both in our lives and in the life of the universe that have not yet been scientifically explained.

For example, Shalila and I don't know why apples taste so delicious or why our solar system functions without error. In spite of this, the apples nourish us and we are gladdened daily by the light of the sun and the sparkle of the stars. To come to these conclusions we require neither scientific proof nor the belief in something. Or would it be better to avoid these things in future, lacking scientific proof and belief. Well, the fact *that* we experience these things is enough for us and we will continue to appreciate them in the future. The experience of Reiki alone will oft suffice to prove its worth, but science and belief also have their role to play. Science for example can confirm the effects that Reiki causes while believing in it can open us up to receive it better and more deeply. Of course, Reiki will function without any preconceptions, but the presence of them won't harm it either. But do not let yourself be deluded. Our thoughts form and influence us far more than we believe. Everything we do with conviction, inner happiness, optimism and dedication will bring about success and fulfillment, no matter what the area of life. This fact plays an inestimable role in all kinds of therapy too, whatever the form. If we are against a form of treatment — whether in our outer life style or inner attitude — we will harm ourselves above all. We can even impede the natural flow of healing to a certain extent by having a negative outlook or attitude.

The fact that our bodies immediately react to our thoughts has been proved by means of simple kinesiological tests, which prove that as soon as we think a negative thought (or find ourselves in a negative situation), the organsim reacts with weakness or reduced vitality. On the other hand, positive thoughts or situations will bring about an increase in vitality and strength. (Instructions for carrying out this easy test can be found in the book "B.K. — Behavioural Kinesiology — your body doesn't lie," by Dr. John Diamond, Harper & Row, 1979 .)

When Goethe said:

'It is the spirit which creates the body,"

he probably had this phenomenon in mind.

Yet it is not only our bodies which we are continually giving shape to. The influence of our spirit affects all aspects of our existence. With our fears and wishes, thoughts and feelings, words and deeds, both conscious and unconscious, we daily forge our lives in the kiln of time.

In this respect, let us consider these words of the Bible:

"Be not deceived, God is not mocked, for whatsoever a man soweth, that shall he also reap."

Galatians 6.7

or these simple proverbs:

"Everyone is the architect of his own future."

and

"As the question, so the answer."

Very instructive information on this theme is to be found in Charles Webster Leadbeater's books, which makes a very significant contribution to a deeper understanding of how Reiki heals on the mental plane (please see chapter 11). In his book, Charles Leadbeater, a theosophist who lived from 1847 to 1943, describes very vividly how our thoughts produce little beings, which he calls "elementals." These thought-beings, which we bring about ourselves, have the desire to stay alive and to grow larger. If we produce a certain kind of thought only very seldom or in a superficial manner, the elemental generated will not be very substantial and will immediately disappear. If we think of something very often or very intensely however, the corresponding elemental will become larger and stronger in accordance and will manage to stay alive for a long time. Thoughts which are similar in character will cluster together into large bunches.

An elemental possesses a certain *freedom of action.* It can take up contact with similar impulses coming from the surroundings in order to fulfill a *"mother-thought,"* such as "I feel fine today." In order to nourish itself and keep alive, the elemental will automatically do everything in its power to have this thought repeated and confirmed. This theory provides a plausible explanation for the great success achieved by various methods of positive thinking.

However, the same mechanism can also be applied to negative thoughts. We all know how difficult it is to break a bad habit or stop repeating a certain thought or thinking about things in a certain way. The moment we try to do this by letting unwanted thoughts pass by unnoticed, the "elemental" in question begins to fear for its life and tries to push us back to the desired way of thinking. (However, if it fails in this, it will become more and more insubstantial and will soon disappear altogether.)

A group of people, a whole race or country, can build up a collective thought being of their own. The effects of such a collective elemental can be quite overwhelming. For example, think of what would happen if the media incorrectly reported the approach of a dangerous flu epidemic, with details of the symptoms. How many people would immediately feel unwell and get it. What would happen, however, were the same people told instead that unusual weather conditions would be increasing their vitality and immunity to illness in the next few days. Would they get the flu after all?

The more people involved in a collectively-produced thought, the greater will be its effect. This effect can be increased further when the thought in question is taken up on a very fine level of consciousness. Just as the finer the form of matter, the more energy there will be present (as in the splitting of the atom for example), so too the deeper the level of consciousness and the closer we are to a state of inner unity with all creation, the more effective our thoughts.

At such a level, new laws come into play, laws which exceed by far the influence of the elementals mentioned above. A thought of love expressed on this finest and deepest level of consciousness, where Divinity is to be found in all beings, will be able to come into contact with the innermost sphere of life itself without needing the agency of an elemental. It is surely superfluous to say that every thought made on this level will automatically be positive.

This principle was first proved scientifically in 1976, when it was observed that the rates for crime, illness and accidents significantly declined in cities where at least 1 % of the population carried out Transcendental Meditation. Today, groups of 7,000 (7,000 being the square root of 1 % of the population of the world) make conscious use of this phenomenon and practise Transcendental Meditation all at the same time in order to further world peace.

The Reiki Association has taken up this idea and recommends the transfer of Reiki in groups in order to support world peace with its healing energy. (Please see chapter 10 for more details.)

These fundamental findings regarding the effects that can be brought about by a united spiritual effort have been confirmed by many well-known physicists and scientists, such as Fritjof Capra and Rupert Sheldrake, who have proved the existence of the above phenomenom with many experiments.

We cite these cases in order to demonstrate that the inner and outer richness of our lives lies in our own hands and that we do not need to look on world affairs with a sense of helplessness.

Today, this knowledge of cause and effect is practical reality for many people. For others, it is still very unusual, but the fact that a point of view is habitual does not mean to say that is the truth. Should you decide to undergo Reiki treatment without being absolutely convinced of the effectiveness of the method, try to take up a neutral attitude of non-judgement. Be curious and wait and see what happens. Even if you do build up a negative thought elemental, it won't affect the ability of Reiki to heal you, but of course an open or positive attitudee will enable Reiki to unfold to its full extent.

The first time Shalila treated her mother, an old woman in her late seventies, she was astonished at the depth of her reaction. She asked her mother about this and was told, "I decided to accept everything you would be giving me with gratitude — and to simply want to get better." Every patient with such a positive attitude will be able to help and support the work of his practitioner in an active way and become his own co-practitioner.

Reiki is not a complicated *technique* and requires neither great effort, talent or ability, it is a method of healing which is absolutely natural and it is this natural flow of life which leads us on to greater perfection, harmony and luck. If you cannot consciously swim with this flow, let yourself at least be carried along by it.

You have probably already fought *against* it many times in the past and cost yourself many pleasant hours in the process. True, you may have achieved a lot this way, but don't forget that fighting always involves separation and isolation from life in its entirety. This does not mean to say that you should become passive or not get involved in things. However, there is a big difference between taking up a cause and fighting for one. In order to see the positive side of things, however, you will have to open yourself up first.

Success

When we think of failure
Failure will be ours.
If we remain undecided
Nothing will ever change.
All we need to do
Is want to achieve something
          great
And then simply to do it.
Never think of failure
For what we think,
Will come about.

                              Maharishi Mahesh Yogi

Take a bite

You don't have to believe in Reiki
For it to have a deep effect on you.
You don't have to believe
That fruit is delicious
In order to enjoy it.
But you'll have to take a bite first.

CHAPTER 5

How to Become a Reiki Channel

Maybe you will one day feel the desire to not only receive Reiki but pass it on to others as well. Maybe you have had Reiki treatment and now want to use it on yourself. What are the basic requirements that have to be fulfilled? The first time Bodo heard about Reiki he immediately registered for the next course. A short description was sufficient and he was convinced that this was the method he had been searching for in vain all the years of his professional work. Shalila on the other hand wanted a "trial treatment" before deciding to attend, while another friend let a whole year go by before reaching the same decision. As you can see, there are no hard and fast rules here either.

Reiki is so easy to carry out that children will learn it in two days. However, the desire to use Reiki for the benefit of yourself and others should be an honest one and not the result of a passing whim or fancy. Once you are quite clear on this, there is nothing to stop you from taking part in a Reiki seminar yourself.

In the original tradition of Reiki there are two Reiki degrees as well as a Master degree. This tradition was represented uniformly by both Reiki organizations until 1983. The First Degree will enable you to transfer Reiki to yourself and others by the laying on of your hands. This degree can be obtained in the weekend course.

Usually 10 to 25 pupils, coming from all walks of life, take part in "First Degree' seminars. Some of them will be medical people but housewives, students and people leading an alternative way of life will also be taking part, both young and old. The atmosphere will be relaxed and the participants will probably become very close during the seminar, something which will be very new to some of them.

The First Degree course usually begins with some introductory explainations and then the first of four initiations (which are carried out by a Reiki teacher) will take place.

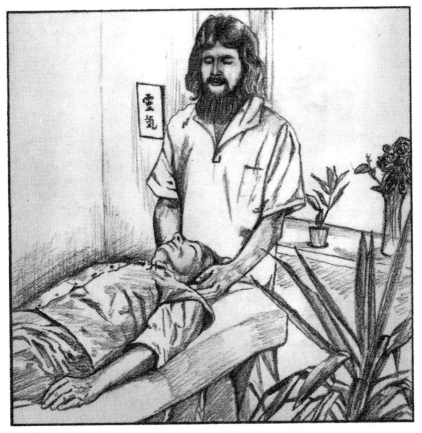

Reiki is not taught like other methods of medicine or healing. We were all born with Reiki in us, for Reiki is the power of life itself. During the four traditional initiation ceremonies an inner healing channel will be opened up within you to attune you to the flow of Reiki energy.

Experiencing this attunement is especially moving for many people, but we are not in a position to give exact details here. Words alone cannot do justice to the experience and they will not open you up to become a Reiki channel either.

Furthermore, there are certain advantages involved in the teacher-pupil relationship inherent to Reiki initiation. For example, you will be able to ask the teacher for his advice if required. Furthermore, your teacher is part of a traditional line of Masters who have preserved the true knowledge of Reiki in its original form over a long period of time, thus guaranteeing both the purity and effectiveness of what you learn.

After the first initiation, Reiki energy will start to flow through your hands. The Master may have told you to put your hands on yourself beforehand and watch what happens. When you do the same thing afterwards, you will notice a definite difference, for a fine form of energy will be flowing through your hands, warm, pleasant and healing.

Between the various initiation stages that follow you will get to know the different ways of placing your hands on a person, which are very easy to learn. Then, to pleasant background music, you will try them out on each other. During these first try-outs some participants may have some very moving experiences while others will simply feel relaxed and harmonious. Afterwards you will tell each other what you experienced and speak to the Master. During the course of the seminar you will notice how the facial expressions of the participants change, how they look younger and more relaxed. Some of them will be positively glowing and a look at yourself in the mirror will reveal two unusually happy eyes gazing back at you. Before the seminar comes to an end, you will be handed out handsome First Degree Certificates and everyone will probably embrace before the group finally breaks up. With the Certificate you will have gained the ability to treat both yourself and others by the laying on of your hands. You will also be able to increase the efficacy of medicine and strengthen the wholesomeness of food, cosmetics etc. with the help of your Reiki energy as well as being able to transfer its healing power to animals and plants as well.

Reiki seminars are now offered at regular intervals in many cities and exact details can be obtained from any of the Reiki Masters. Get further detailed information from the Associations. That way you will know their differences and schedules. Then you can decide what suits you best.

If you can get ten people or more together who are interested in doing such a course in your neighborhood, a Reiki Master may be prepared to come and hold one for you. In this case a collapsible massage table and a woolen blanket should be brought along, if available. Loose, natural clothing is to be recommended, not only during but also after the course.

Once you have obtained the First Degree a time of trying Reiki out will begin. Almost everybody knows someone he'd like to treat — the baby of his sister, the grandmother with the broken hip, the young girl having problems with her period, the colleague with his habitual bad moods and the neighbor's dog which has been limping around for several days.

This is an important time and you should make good use of it. Whoever works in a clinic or practice will have enough opportunity to do so anyway. After a short period the first "miracles" will start to happen and many a deep and pleasant experience will come about through the healing power of your hands. Never forget that this healing force is not of your own, however, and above all, remain modest. You never know how things will work out next time.

You should also take note of one important fact: the more Reiki you give, the stronger will be the energy flowing through your hands. Therefore, use Reiki as often as you can, to your own benefit and to that of others.

Should you not use Reiki for a longer period of time, however, do not worry. You will stay a Reiki channel all your life even if you make no use of it for thirty years on end. Isn't this truly wonderful?

When you treat others, you will start to feel the effects of Reiki on yourself, too. Fundamental changes will set in and new things will start to develop. You will find it easier to cast off old, outlived structures and you will notice

that you are being led and guided more and more. At the same time, repressed experiences may come back to the surface, meaning that the time has come to resolve them, which is not always very pleasant. The speed of these new developments may be too fast for some and they will want to lay Reiki "to one side" for a while. For example, a friend of ours had very definite Kundalini experiences after treating someone with Reiki a few times. (Kundalini is the energy which rises up through the spinal chord.) At the same time, her backache, which was familiar to her from long courses of meditation, made itself felt again. She decided to stop giving Reiki to others for a few days and to concentrate on herself. After a while, the symptoms began to disappear and she soon felt as new as if she had stepped out of a refreshing bath. If you find yourself in such a situation, just follow your inner feelings. Usually the developments you will experience when you begin to do Reiki will take place very harmoniously, but be prepared for both growth and change to occur and be ready to accept what comes about. Once you have gathered experience for a few weeks or months you may want to learn new aspects of Reiki or increase the effectivity of your treaments. This can be achieved by obtaining the Second Reiki Degree. Here it will be the Master, however, who will decide who is to take part in such a course and who should continue working with First Degree Reiki a little longer.

These courses usually last several days and there is more that has to be learned. You will be working with some of the symbols discovered by Dr. Usui, which have to be memorized since you are not allowed to write them down. The groups involved are smaller and usually consist of only five people. After the single initiation ceremony you will be able to:

1. intensify the effect of your treatments.
2. heal according to the "mental" method and
3. carry out absentee healing (i.e., you will be able to heal without needing direct bodily contact).

(Absentee healing and the "mental" method will be treated in chapters 10 and 11 respectively.)

Second Degree Reiki grants you greater flexibility while increasing the effectiveness of treatment to a considerable extent. Information regarding the Second Degree and dates of courses can be obtained from your Reiki Master.

After you have obtained the Second Degree, you may feel the wish one day to teach Reiki to others and open them up to become channels themselves. Not many Reiki practitioners tread this path, but it is one that is linked with much fulfillment and growth as well as having a special blessing of its own.

The fee for the Master Degree is in both organizations very high. This large sum of money is a final hurdle in proving the worth of an aspirant to the Master title. When one considers that disciples often used to spend years or even decades living in seclusion with a master before receiving spiritual initiation, we are of the opinion that the amount we have to give today in exchange for what we receive is of equivalent value and therefore appropriate.

The Reiki Alliance continues the traditional teaching of two degrees and a Master's degree, while since 1983 the A.I.R.A. (now T.R.T.A.I.) has made changes and modifications in the way of teaching in the division and number of degrees and as in the naming of Reiki and their organization. If you would like to be informed about the current situation, please contact the organization directly. (See addresses at end of book.)

CHAPTER 6

Introduction to Practical Work with Reiki

We would now like to mention some general rules and principles which should be observed when giving Reiki.

During the First Degree seminar you will have learned various positions which are useful for giving treatment. There are about 10-20 basic positions altogether and a few additional ones for special cases. They are so logical and easy to carry out that they can be memorized by anyone in a couple of days. You will also be given a few sketches during most courses which will help refresh your memory, when necessary, while giving details of positions which have proved useful in the case of certain complaints and illnesses.

These positions do not have to be carried out exactly as shown and it is not necessary to keep to the exact sequence either, although doing so will entail certain advantages. For example, you won't have to keep wondering which position comes next, or whether one has been forgotten, while you are treating a patient but will be free to concentrate on the patient and the way you are treating him.

Many Reiki Masters advise letting yourself be guided by your inner feeling and allowing your hands to go where they intuitively want to during a treatment. It will also usually be right to transfer Reiki at points where the patient feels pain. Therefore, it is not necessary to keep to a rigid system without deviation.

When you begin a series of treatments, you should try to give four treatments on four successive days at the beginning. These will, above all, stimulate the body to cleanse itself of poisons. We, therefore, recommend patients drink a lot of water or tea during this time in order to support the natural detoxication reactions which set in.

Always try to carry out all the basic positions when you give a treatment and leave problematical areas to the end, when they can be treated more intensively. As a rule, each position should be held for three to five minutes. In

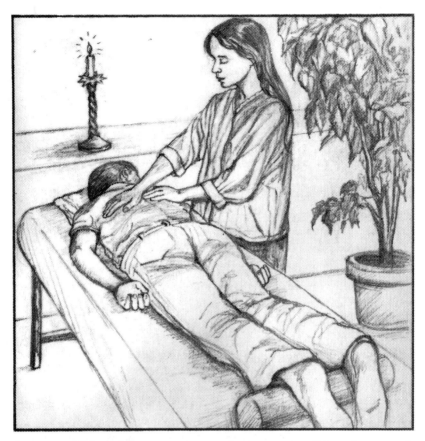

time you will feel when a zone has received enough Reiki, and you won't need to keep an eye on the time any more. Problematical areas can be treated for 10 to 20 minutes. Plan enough time for treatment and make sure that it can come to an end harmoniously. A period of at least one hour will generally be necessary. In the case of the old or very ill, treatment should not last longer than 20 to 30 minutes at first, but this can be increased with time if necessary. Ten to 20 minutes will generally be sufficient for babies and small children.

And now a few tips:

○ Take off your watch and rings before treatment.
○ Wash your hands under running water both before and after every treatment.

○ Let the patient take off his shoes and loosen tight clothing such as belt, tie, waistband, brassiere etc. Since Reiki energy will pass through clothing, belts, bandages and plaster casts, other items of clothing will not need to be taken off.

○ It is very important for the patient to not cross his legs during treatment since this may block the flow of energy.

○ The patient should let his arms lay loosely next to his body. When he is lying on his stomach he can fold them under his head.

○ When you lay your hands on the patient, do so gently.

○ If the patient's body cannot be touched, as in the case of burns, it will be sufficient to hold your hands a few centimeters above it. (Reiki will work just as effectively up to 2 inches away from the body.)

○ Keep your fingers closed during treatment.

○ Hold every position for three to five minutes.

In case you don't always feel the familiar warm "flowing" sensation, this does not mean to say that the Reiki energy is not present. It will simply be adapting itself to the needs of the patient.

After treatment, your patient should try to rest a while, if possible. This may be an important time for him, a time when things which came into movement during treatment can continue to pulse and vibrate afterwards with a chance of being resolved. If you feel the wish to express thanks for the Reiki energy you have or are to receive, this can be done before or after treatment. Above all, never forget the more Reiki you give, the stronger will be the flow of Reiki energy within you. We wish you much joy in being a Reiki channel.

Chapter 7

Treating Yourself

There is probably no other method of self-treatment as simple and as effective as Reiki. You can give yourself treatment wherever you are, because Reiki is always with you, and you won't need any special aids or devices either. Whenever you feel pain somewhere, or get into a bad state, when you are tired, worked up or simply scared, you will be able to calm yourself down immediately and relax with your Reiki energy and use it to strengthen and harmonize yourself again.

However, you should not limit treating yourself to unusual situations. Once you have achieved the First Reiki Degree you can charge up your "battery of life" daily by giving Reiki to yourself. In this way many illnesses will not be able to develop, and you will be spared much trouble. Your spiritual growth will be furthered and your life will take on another quality.

Many people who take part in Reiki seminars do it solely because of the possibility of self-treatment. For some, Reiki is a natural alternative to usual medical methods, while others find that they begin to sleep deeply and peacefully again. Many will now be able to free themselves of pain and illness, weakness and suffering, both physical and mental.
Something interesting happened to Shalila soon after her first Reiki course. At the time she was having intestinal problems, and so she laid her hands on her stomach each evening before going to sleep to give herself Reiki. A few days later she discovered that a large, dark wart she had had on her stomach since childhood had fallen off, leaving behind a pink area as proof of its ever having existed. She had simply wanted to treat her intestinal problem, and now her familiar but ugly wart had disappeared. She was delighted, of course. This is but another example of how little we can consciously direct the flow of Reiki energy, even when we treat ourselves. Here, too, we are only channels which this energy flows through.
In principle, you can treat yourself with the same holds you use for treating

patients, and all the basic rules that apply to the treating of patients hold true here, too. The treatment of one's own upper back poses more of a problem, however, and some people also have difficulty in reaching their feet, but once you have obtained Second Degree Reiki you will be able to treat these areas with the absentee technique. This may sound like a joke at first, but it works very well. Of course, the "mental" technique can also be used for treating yourself.

We would now like to describe a short means of self-treatment. Lie or sit down comfortably, and starting with your head, lay your hands gently in the various head positions and let the Reiki energy flow. Now, slowly work your way down down the rest of your body. You should include your heart, your liver, your spleen, stomach and solar plexus as well as the lower stomach area and the kidneys, too, if possible. Each position should be held for three

to five minutes. Problematical areas can be treated for 10 to 20 minutes or as long as seems right. You can also let your hands move to positions they are innerly guided to, as you would do when you treat a patient, and of course you can place them on areas that particularly hurt. Self-treatment is extremely effective when carried out before falling asleep, too, for it programs the night's rest for a peaceful and relaxed sleep.

These are just some of the ways you can treat yourself. You will probably find out new ways of your own very quickly.

Chapter 8

A Quick Means of Treatment

It may happen that you find yourself in a situation one day where you would
like to give someone Reiki but cannot, because there simply isn't enough
time. Maybe your daughter or a friend of yours comes to you half an hour
before a test and wants to feel the soothing effect of your Reiki hands, or
someone travelling with you in a train compartment suddenly feels unwell.

Maybe you are pressed for time yourself but don't want to turn someone in search of help away. In all these cases you can resort to a quick form of treatment which includes all the most important Reiki positions. Although it is better to give a complete course of treatment, there are times when a short one is better than none at all. However, never give your patient the impression that you are in a hurry. Simply make use of the short time available to you and remain peaceful and tranquil in mood. Even a short treatment can bring about wonderful results, maybe because we don't have such high expectations as we do before a normal length treatment:

Instructions for carrying out a quick treatment

The patient should be seated if posssible.

1st position: *Gently lay your hands on your patient's shoulders.*
2nd position: *Gently lay them on the top of his head.*
3rd position: *Lay one hand on the Medulla oblongata (the area between the back of the head and the top of the spine) and the other on the forehead.*
4th position: *Lay one hand on the seventh (protruding) cervical vertibrae and the other in the pit of the throat.*
5th position: *Lay one hand on the breastbone and the other on the back at the same height.*
6th position: *Lay one hand on the solar plexus (stomach) and the other at the same height on the back.*
7th position: *Lay one hand on the lower stomach and the other at the bottom of the back at the same height.*

Reiki has also proved to be excellent as an additional means of giving first aid in the case of accidents and shock. Here you should immediately lay one hand onto the solar plexus and the other onto the kidneys (suprarenal glands). Once you have done this, move the second hand to the outer edge of the shoulders.

Chapter 9

Using Reiki for Babies

There is hardly a more natural and pleasant way of giving Reiki than for a mother to give it to her baby. A mother often holds her baby lovingly anyway and once she has learned to give Reiki she can pass it on to her baby each time she strokes and touches it. This higher form of energy will intensify the natural relationship between mother and child and make it finer. Moreover, everything the infant human being experiences in its first weeks, months and years condition it for life. Whoever received a lot of love and affection as a baby will generally be able to pass on these qualities himself when he is older. Reiki is not only a method of healing, it is also a special form of love that all babies thrive on.

A mother-to-be can pass Reiki onto the child within her and favorably influence the course of his life to come. Later, when something is wrong with the little being entrusted to her care, such a mother will never have to feel helpless, but will always be able to give her child the right kind of healing energy in every situation. After all, isn't it is a normal instinct anyway to soothe and touch a child when it has hurt itself?

Although Reiki can be used for every little ache and pain, it will also support the process of healing in cases of serious illness, too. In every event it will have a positive and healing effect, will generally soothe a fretful patient and has proved its worth as an aid for falling asleep.

Moreover, when parents treat their children themselves, they are able to shoulder part of the responsibility usually entrusted to doctors and hospitals alone, as well as having the chance to grow and develop with their children through the illness.

Of course, it is possible to treat babies and children that are not your own but it is always better for mothers (and fathers) to treat their children themselves, since the contact between them is a natural one. When a strange person treats a child, he will generally have to win its trust first.

We, therefore, recommend you to tell mothers who bring their babies to you for treatment that the ideal solution would be for them to take part in a Reiki

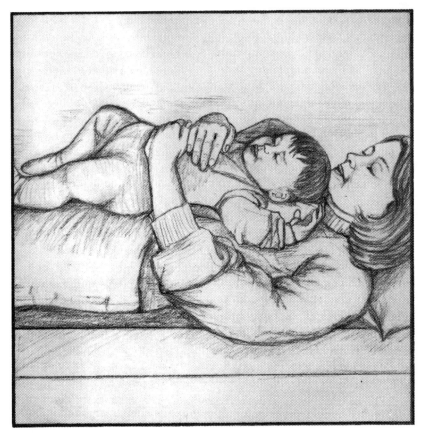

seminar themselves. This is a more satisfying solution in the long run as well as being less complicated and considerably cheaper. Moreover, such a mother will be able to treat not only her baby but also the rest of the family with Reiki.

While we were visiting Asia, many mothers brought us their babies for treatment, simply because there were no doctors in many of the areas we were staying in. In the process, we found out that it was easiest to treat babies when their mothers were nursing them (still a common sight in many Asian countries), for babies feel safe and protected in the most natural possible way when they are being nursed.

Treatment of babies and small children should not take as long as that of adults. Sometimes a few minutes will be sufficient, but ten to twenty minutes will be more appropriate in more difficult cases. You just need to go by feeling. The reaction of the child will tell you when it has had enough. When babies stretch their toes, they are signalling, "I am paying attention to what is going on."

The absentee healing method can also be used for babies and toddlers, for example when you have to make a journey and leave the child at home or when you hear it crying in another room. The mental healing technique is another possibility which is pleasant to use in such cases, especially when there are psychic problems such as fearfulness, bed-wetting, fitfulness, etc. Every now and then people ask us about the effect of Reiki on congenital faults, such as down syndrom. Unfortunately, we have no experience in this field but it can be expected that treating such a child with Reiki will lead to development along natural, positive lines. Such a treatment would have to be carried out over a longer period of time as a rule, however, and it would be best if the parents themselves were to carry it out.

In this respect we would like to mention "Pre-natal Therapy" (otherwise known as the "Metamorphic Method"*), a very natural method which has proved extremely suitable in the treatment of disturbances caused before birth. Like Reiki, this method is simple to use and is especially helpful for the parents of mongoloid children, for example. A carefully thought-out combination of Reiki, which passes on universal life energy, and Pre-natal Therapy, which helps dissolve blockages which were developed before birth, will be ideal in such cases.

If it is true that the love and affection we invest in our children will bear fruit in the next generation, how much more does the same apply to Reiki? And so, in yet another way, Reiki can make an important contribution towards the creation of a new and more positive age.

---

* "Metamorphosis — a Textbook on Pre-natal Therapy" by Robert St. John, Ojai (Cal), 1980
"The Metamorphic Technique, Principles and Practice" by Gaston St. Pierre and Debbie Boater, Element Books Ltd., England

A life without love

Belief without love will make you fanatical,
Duty without love will make you ill-humored,
Order without love will make you pedantic,
Power without love will make you violent,
Justice without love will make you severe,
A life without love will make you ill.

Chapter 10

Absentee Healing With Reiki

Many people react incredulously or are at least taken aback when we tell them that Reiki can be passed on to other people over a long distance. However, in our day and age, the possibility of this should not surprise or amaze us. For example, we know from radio and television that waves can be sent through the ether and made audible or visible once they have been picked up by the right kind of receiver. Every single one of us is familiar with this "wire-less" form of transmission.

Thanks to investigation methods developed by modern medical technology, we know today that our brains produce frequencies which differ according to the kind of brain activity causing them. Our thoughts are nothing other than vibratory patterns which are transmitted by our brains, and, like radio waves, they can be picked up by the right kind of receiver.

Many people have become acquainted with the phenomenom of telepathy without being aware of it. How often do you think of something and then someone else says it. Sometimes, too, we sense that someone we love is thinking intensely of us, or we are aware that something is happening to a member of the family living far away. If this can happen with thoughts, why can it not happen with the healing energy of Reiki?

However, we know that not every thought we send out automatically reaches its intended recipient and, likewise, it is not sufficient to just send someone Reiki in our thoughts, either. Instead, we have to use a technique which functions as perfectly as calling someone up on the telephone. When we do this, for example, it doesn't matter if a professor, a grandmother or a little girl makes the call. So long as the correct number is dialed, the telephone will ring at the other end. Although this has nothing to do with black magic or hocus-pocus, what would a person from the Middle Ages think? Wouldn't a telephone seem like magic to him? And yet the laws of physics, which enable us to make telephone calls in our day and age, were also in existence during the Middle Ages and had simply not yet been discovered and put to use.

In much the same way, natural laws also exist which enable us to transfer life energy over a long distance, and, even though they have not yet been discovered and confirmed by modern-day science, they do exist. Furthermore, there have always been people who were aware that they existed, people who have developed methods for making successful use of them. The Reiki method of absentee healing is based on these laws and the key to them, which was discovered by Dr. Ursui, can be learned in Second Degree Reiki. To keep to our example of the telephone, it is not necessary, however, to know all the natural laws responsible for this phenomenon to be able to make use of it.

Absentee healing can be put to use when you cannot physically be with the person needing treatment, such as someone lying in hospital or living in a distant town. It is also a method which can immediately put to use when you are asked for treatment by letter or telephone.

People who have never had a Reiki treatment at all will be skeptical about absentee healing at first. However, once they have had a "normal" treatment, they will usually open up in their attitude to this kind of experiment.

Once you have arranged to treat a patient via the absentee method, it will be important to arrange a time when you will both have some peace and quiet. This will generally be in the evenings. Like direct treatment, absentee healing should be carried out on four successive days. The recipient should not be active during the arranged time but should sit or, more preferably, lie down. Make a note of the time arranged and make sure that the recipient knows it, too. In case you do a lot of absentee healing, it will be necessary to plan your appointments conscientiously, otherwise the same will happen to you as did to us while we were giving a lecture. The lecture had been arranged at very short notice and right in the middle of it, it suddenly occurred to us that we had forgotten that we had an absentee treatment for the same evening and that there were only ten minutes to go before the treatment was due to begin. Luckily we were giving the lecture together, and so Shalila was able to go into an adjoining room and carry the treatment out herself, saving us from a very awkward situation.

A proper appointment book will help you to avoid the same kind of thing happening to you. Printed appointment cards are also useful, especially when details of your name and address are included, so that the patient can cancel in time, if necessary. Always make a note of both the Christian and surname of your patients, for you will need these to carry out absentee healing. If the patient is unknown to you, a characterisitc photograph of him or her will be necessary, or at least very helpful. This photograph should be placed at your disposal at the beginning of treatment, complete with details of the full name. However, in urgent cases we have been able to treat successfully with nothing more than a general description of the person involved.

After the first four (or three) successive treatments have been carried out, further ones can then be arranged. A series of treatment can last for several weeks, or even months if necessary. In this case it is advantageous to send Reiki to the recipient at the same time on the same day of the week. This way both sides will find the times easier to keep to.

The results of absentee treatment are in no way inferior to those attained by the direct method, although patients will usually feel the effects of the latter more distinctly. In both cases, the energy will be the same. Many practitioners can feel the flow of Reiki energy in the various parts of the patient's body when they are treating with the absentee method, while others develop a very clear feeling of what is wrong with the patient and how treatment should be carried out.

One advantage of absentee healing will obviously be the fact that you do not need a special place to do it — a comfortable place to sit down will be all you need. Also, it does not take up as much time as the "direct" method. Generally 15 to 20 minutes will suffice, although this can vary. Some Reiki Masters also point out that it is possible to treat a large group of people at the same time by this method.

It won't always be necessary but it will certainly do no harm for the patient to attune himself to the treatment while it is going on and to let himself flow and be carried along by the stream of energy. You should never carry out an absentee treatment against the will of a person, however. Everybody has not only the right to be healthy but also to be ill, and it is our place to respect this. When two or more practitioners unite to send a patient Reiki over a distance, it will be advisable for him to lie down, because the effect can sometimes be very strong.

Someone taking part in a Reiki seminar once related the following incident: She had made an appointment with a practitioner for an absentee treatment but when the appointed time came round, she did not pay much attention to the fact and continued to clean her apartment. She was in the middle of vacuuming when she suddenly felt an unknown sensation that was so strong she could hardly straighten up. When she later called up her Reiki practitioner, he told her that he had been treating her during this time. This incident impressed her so much that she decided to take part in the seminar she was now visiting.

We have also had interesting experiences with the absentee method. Once an

American friend asked us to send Reiki to his mother who had had a serious operation and who was not recovering very well. She didn't recognize her children any more, wasn't aware of what had happened to her and was dull and generally bewildered. We began sending Reiki over to America and a little while later she unexpectedly began to get better. She could think clearly again and was able to take care of herself.

Animals can also be treated by the absentee method, as an interesting case shows. A friend of ours was living on a nearby farm when one of the cows was stricken with a mysterious illness. The cow wouldn't eat anything at all and blood was coming out of its anus. The vet could neither explain the case nor find of a remedy for it, and the animal died a few days later. In the meantime, another cow got the illness and had to be slaughtered. Then Max, the young bull, began to fever and get the same symptoms as well. This was when our friend called us up for help. What we did not know, however, was

that during the telephone call, Max was being picked up to be brought to the slaughter-house. So, knowing nothing and being totally unbiased, we began treating Max and the remaining cows the very same evening with the absentee method in the hope they would be spared this mysterious illness. Five days later the telephone rang again and we were told that Max had just been brought back from the slaughter-house. The livestock dealer wasn't able to tell the astonished farmer how Max had regained his health and none of the other cows caught the disease after this.

As already mentioned, you can also treat yourself by this method for example, when you want to treat your back for example. You do this in exactly the same way as treating someone else over a long distance, and it is a good way of practising the technique.

As is always the case when we treat someone with Reiki, we feel very happy when we have given an absentee treatment, which we generally do together because of the greater effectiveness. Then we look at each other and laugh for inner joy, and then we tell each other what we experienced during the treatment. It never ceases to amaze us just how exactly our reports coincide.

Chapter 11

The Mental Method

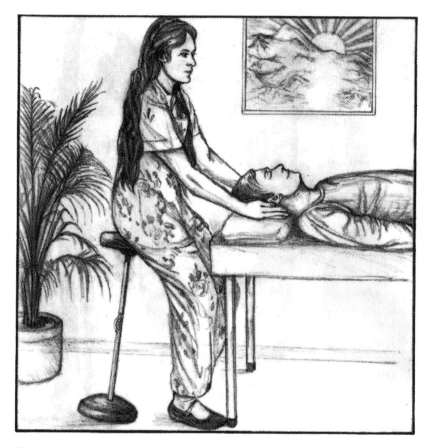

Negative experiences frequently condition our attitude to life and our behaviour. This kind of unconscious programing makes us attract the same distressful experiences over and over again, almost in confirmation of our worst hopes. It is often very difficult to free ourselves of such ingrained patterns of behaviour, even when we know the causes. Here the mental healing method, which is taught in Second Degree Reiki, can be of great help. (The word "mental" is derived from the latin "mens," which has the meaning of "to think," "the thinker," "consciousness" and "concerning the spirit." "Mens" also corresponds to the Sanskrit "manas" from which the word "man" is derived.)

With the help of the right kind of "key," it is possible to come into contact with the innermost being of a person and to change his inner "program" in such a way that his misdirected energy will be transformed and set free. In this way, depression can be changed into the joy of life, and fear will become trust. Lack of courage will turn into optimism and an inferiority complex can be transformed into inner wealth. Hate will become love and happiness, and a positive attitude will arise out of negativity.

The patient will often gain insight into his behaviour and recognize the cause of his problems with the help of the mental method. Moreover, it will also help him to recognize and follow his goal in life more easily.

Since physical illness is usually a manifestation of spiritual inbalance, the mental healing method can be used in the case of all psychic disturbances. In order to help you identify programs which often occur with certain kinds of ailments, we have described the mental and spiritual causes of individual illnesses in chapter 26. Other typical "programs" which will help you in your work are also described to you by your Reiki Master during the Second Degree seminar. Some practitioners can sense their patient's programs intuitively.

Like self-treatment and absentee healing, the mental technique is usually given as part of a normal Reiki treatment and only lasts a few minutes.

However, this form of treatment requires a great sense of responsibility on the part of the practitioner. A lot of thought should go into giving it, and it should only be carried out with the patient's permission. Here, as elsewhere, the practioner should not project his own ideas and value judgements onto his patient. Instead, his sole consideration should be his well-being.

The mental method can also be applied to plants and animals and is a truly wonderful and beneficient instrument with which you will be able to achieve many positive results.

If you want to heal the body, you must first heal the mind.

Plato, 427 — 347 B.C.

Chapter 12

Balancing out the Chakras

Balancing out the chakras with the help of Reiki is not part of the usual program of treatment. However, it is very effective and some practitioners would not want to do without it. The following some basic information on chakras will help you reach a better understanding of the subject. The word "chakra" is derived from Sanskrit and means "wheel," and the chakras themselves are circular energy centers which exist in man's subtle body. Their function and appearance have been described again and again, especially by Eastern cultures.

Most schools of philosophy and esoterics describe seven main chakras and four subsidiary ones, all existing in the subtle body which is the non-material counterpart of our physical one. This subtle body pervades and permeates the physical body and is the energetical basis of all manifestations on the physical level. Clairvoyants perceive chakras as being circular spirals of energy which differ in size and activity from person to person. The chakras are connected to a fine channel of energy which runs parallel to the spinal chord, and our material bodies could not exist without them. Chakras both take up and collect Prana present in the atmosphere and transform and pass on energy. They serve as gateways for the flow of energy and life into our physical bodies.

Each chakra is associated with a certain part of the body and a certain organ which it provides with the energy it needs to function. The seven main chakras correspond to the seven main glands of the endocrine system.

Just as every organ in the human body has its equivalent on the mental and spiritual level, so too every chakra corresponds to a specific aspect of human behaviour and development. The lower chakras are associated with fundamental emotions and needs, for the energy here vibrates at a lower frequency and is therefore cruder in nature. The finer energy of the upper chakras corresponds to man's higher mental and spiritual aspirations and faculties.

A blockage in the energy flow of the chakras as well as an excess of energy can lead to inbalance and disharmony on the physical, mental and spiritual level. Such disturbances are often caused by psychological stress and trauma as well as by painful experiences or an excess of joy.

The chakras are provided with fine antennae which react to every influence coming from outside and which can open up or draw together accordingly. For this reason, the individual chakras in most people vibrate at different frequencies. In normal, undisturbed conditions, the chakras harmonize.

A healer can do a lot by simply "purifying" the chakras and balancing them out so that the energy flows again without disturbance. All meditation and yoga systems seek to balance out the energy of the chakras by purifying the lower energies and guiding them upwards.

In the average person the chakras look like dully glowing little circles of about 2 inches in diameter. However, once awakened in a spiritually developed person, they will pulse and glow and an enormous amount of great energy will flow though them.
We would now like to describe the seven main chakras:

1. *The Root or Base Chakra* lies in the area of the coccyx in men and between the ovaries in women. This chakra is the seat of physical vitality and the fundamental urge to survive. It regulates those mechanisms which keep the physical body alive.
   Glands: the suprarenal glands.
   Organs: the kidneys, the bladder and the spine.

2. *The Sacral or Sexual Chakra* is positioned slightly below the navel, in front of the sacrum (os sacrum). It is the center of sexual energy (both as transmitter and receiver) and of the ego. The feelings of other people are directly perceived with this chakra, making it one of the centers of extra-sensory perception.
   Glands: the gonads.
   Organs: the organs of reproduction and the legs.

3. *The Solar Plexus Chakra* lies slightly above the navel. It is the actual center of the body, the place where physical energy is distributed. It is also the center of unrefined emotions and the power urge and it is here that we "regard our navels." When we are scared, we can feel this area tightening up.
   Gland: the pancreas.
   Organs: the stomach, liver and gall-bladder.

4. *The Heart Chakra* is positioned in the middle of the chest at the height of the heart. It is the center of real, unconditional affection as well as brotherliness, spiritual growth, compassion, devotion and love. Many Eastern methods of meditation are especially designed to open up this chakra.
   Gland: the thymus.
   Organs: the heart, the liver, the lungs and blood circulation.

5. *The Throat Chakra* , also known as the Thyroid or Laryngeal Chakra, is the chakra of communication, self-expression and creativity. This is where you hear your inner voice and ones coming from extrasensory realms.

Gland: the thyroid gland.
Organs: the throat, upper lungs, arms and digestive tract.

6. *The Third Eye Chakra* lies in the middle of the forehead, a little higher than the eyebrows. It is is the center of such forms of extra-sensory perception such as clairvoyance and telepathy. It is the seat of the will, the intellect and the spirit; it is here that we visualize things. The opening of the Third Eye corresponds to spiritual awakening in many mystic traditions.
   Gland: the pituitary gland (the hypohysis).
   Organs, the spine, the lower brain, the left eye, the nose and the ears.

7. *The Crown, or Lotus Chakra* is positioned at the top of the head, at the fontanel. This chakra represents the highest level of consciousness that mankind can attain, known as enlightenment, consciousness of unity and the consciousness of "I am." (For this reason a spiritually awakened person is often represented with a halo or rays of light around his head.) This chakra is the seat of intuition and direct spiritual vision which exceeds the ability of clairvoyance by far.
   Gland: the pineal gland (the epiphysis).
   Organs: the upper brain and the right eye.

If you wish to harmonize the chakras with the help of Reiki, a deeper knowledge of the way they function will not necessarily be required, for the energy of Reiki functions in its own, optimal way. It is therefore very easy to practise this form of Reiki. You can balance out the energy of the chakras by laying your hands on each of them successively, beginning with the Third Eye Chakra for example and working your way down to the Root Chakra or vice versa. A further possibility would be to lay one hand on the Third Eye Chakra and the other on the Root Chakra and then to move your hands to the Throat Chakra and the Sacral Chakra, the Heart Chakra and the Solar Plexus Chakra successively.

Always leave your hands in position until you can feel the same amount or kind of energy flowing through them. For people who live in their heads too much, you can lay one hand on the Third Eye Chakra and, leaving it there, move your other hand from one lower chakra to the other, beginning with the Root Chakra, to balance them out. We do not touch the highest chakra, the Lotus Chakra, when we do this form of treatment, since the highest state of consciousness requires neither harmonization nor the provision of additional energy.

Once you have obtained Second Degree Reiki you will also be able to treat the chakras with the symbols you have learned. They can also be treated with the mental and absentee methods.

Balancing out the chakras will harmonize the body, dissolve blockages of energy and set potential capabilities free. Make use of this special form of Reiki treatment whenever appropriate. It will be worth it.

Chapter 13

The Aura

"Aura" is a Latin word meaning "gently moving air," "a breath of air," "fragrance," "light" and " a glow of light." The aura itself is an energy field which surrounds the body and permeates it, like a kind of halo. It is referred to by Baron Reichenbach as an "odic radiant sheathe". It consists of the seven auras which belong to man's seven subtle energy bodies. Generally, a distinction is made between

1. the *spiritual aura* which has a diameter of 15 to 18 feet;
2. the *mental aura,* which usually has a diameter of up to eight feet; and
3. the *etheric aura,* which radiates from the physical body to a length of about eight inches.

Since the auras overlap, it is not always possible to determine them individually. What clairvoyants usually see, however, is the etheric aura. This is perceived as being a kind of translucent field consisting of different colors and patterns. The aura can change in color, size, structure and intensity according to the mental and emotional state of the person involved. Strongly-felt emotions and physical and mental illness will be reflected by the appearance of the aura. In an analysis made by the British Colour Council, the aura was determined as possessing over 4,700 individually registered shades. Not only human beings but also plants, animals and stones have auras.

The fact that these fields of energy do not exist solely in the imagination of a few people has been proved scientifically by Kirlian photography*, a special method which makes the aura visible. Of significance in this context is a form of diagnosis developed by the West German natural health practi-

---

* "The Kirlian Aura" by Stanley Krippner and Daniel Rubin

tioner Peter Mandel, who makes use of Kirlian photography in his so-called Energy Emission Analysis.**

Since we only intend to deal with the aura here in terms of healing with Reiki, further literature has been listed below for those interested.

We would now like to describe a very easy method of harmonizing the aura and smoothing it out, which is not part of the traditional program of Reiki treatment but which has proved to be so successful that several Reiki Masters now recommend it. You can incorporate it into your own program of treatment, of course, but it can also be done at any time. We ourselves carry it out before and after we give Reiki.

In order to harmonize the aura (which you do not have to see in order to practise this method successfully) let your patient lie on his back and, facing him, stand to his left. Now with your right hand, make a wide elliptical movement 8 inches above the patient, from head to foot and back again. Repeat three times. You may or may not feel a slight resistance when you touch the aura. This will have to do with the fact that we have been conditioned for most our lives to only believe in what we can see and feel. However, whether you feel the aura or not, your treatment will be equally effective and once you have started to "look out" for the aura, you will probably begin to "feel" it after a while.

This method can also be carried out at the end of every Reiki session, when the patient is lying on his stomach. Here again, stand to the right of the patient and describe three ellipses in the air above his body, from head to foot and back again, that is all. This method will generally require no more than 12 seconds and will leave the patient feeling in a good way as well as harmonizing him. Very sensitive people will feel their auras being smoothed out very distinctly.

There is also a method for loosening up the aura, which can be done at any time but not as part of a Reiki session. It is very effective and helpful, especially when someone is depressed or weighed down. In this method the patient should stand in front of you with his eyes closed. Now, starting at the feet and working your way up, loosen up the aura as if you were whirling feathers into the air. Repeat from all sides, until the whole aura has been treated. This method will cheer people up and help them feel freer. Try it out sometime.

** Peter Mandel: Energy Emission Analysis, Life Rhythm 1987, Mendocino, CA.

Chapter 14

The Thymus Gland

The term "thymus" is derived from the Greek word *thymos,* which means life-force or vitality. We would now like to mention a simple technique involving the thymus gland which will increase your own inner life-force. Once again, this is not part of the traditional Reiki system of treatment and it is also not taught by Reiki Masters in connection with Reiki either.

However, we have included it here because it is extremely simple and effective. Since it can be combined with Reiki very well it can be included in your program of treatment if you wish.

The thymus gland is situated in the middle of the chest, behind the upper part of the breast-bone. The more we know about the thymus gland, the more significant its functioning in an overall sense appears to be. Until a short time ago, the thymus gland was held to be harmful or at best, superfluous. Today we know that the thymus is the most important organ in the maintenance of our immunological system. It has also become an increasingly important factor in the prevention and treatment of cancer.

Today, we also know that the thymus gland is weakened in about 95 of humanity. However, thousands of simple kinesiological muscle tests, as taught and practised in the "Applied Kinesiology" and "Touch for Health"* methods, prove that a weakened thymus gland can be strengthened within a matter of seconds. This is done by knocking lightly against the thymus with your fingertips or fist 10 or 20 times, in whatever rhythm you care to choose. (Rubbing the thymus will weaken it however.) Knocking the thymus will stabilize your system and fill you with vitality in a matter of seconds. Of course, you can also lay your hands on the thymus and provide it with Reiki energy. As the tests mentioned before demonstrate, this is a further effective means of putting Reiki to use.

If you strengthen your thymus regularly every morning — and as often as you feel like it during the course of the day —
you will soon feel definitely stronger. Although this method may sound deceptively simple, it is extremely positive and far-reaching in effect and one that you can recommend to your patients.

---

* "B.K. Behavioural Kinesiology — your body doesn't lie", by Dr.John Diamond, Warner Books, 1980

Chapter 15

Team Treatment

A very pleasant way of sharing the happiness and joy you experience when you treat someone with Reiki is to treat with other practitioners at the same time. This method not only increases the effectiveness of treatment, it is also shorter while being a lot more enjoyable. Bodo once took part in a session involving no fewer than twelve practitioners and one patient, who enjoyed it very much. Dr. Hayashi, the former Grand Master, also let his patients be treated by several practitioners at once in his Reiki clinic in Tokyo. Shalila and I always try to treat our patients together whenever possible.

Before commencing treatment, it is important to decide who should start off and which sequence should be followed, but this is not something to discuss in front of the patient. In the case of Shalila and myself, a few glances will suffice and we will begin, one starting at the head and the other at the upper part of the body. Then we continue with the treatment until our glances meet again over the patient.

When we treat together, we usually need a little more than half an hour. Treating with several practitioners at once has proved especially valuable in difficult and stubborn cases and, for this reason, it is a good idea to keep in touch with other practitioners. After team treatment, it is also a good idea to sit round a cup of tea for a while and talk "shop." This way you can pass on experiences you have made with Reiki and exchange ideas. In this way, we can also support and help each other on our path through life, strengthened by the knowledge of its deeper meaning.

Chapter 16

The Reiki Circle

As C.G. Jung once pointed out, we have become more and more estranged from traditional symbols*, which once possessed such great meaning and which have since lost their effectiveness for us. However, when you take part in a large meeting of Reiki practitioners, you will be able to fill the ancient symbol of the circle with new life again.

The circle stands for infinity and perfection and by forming one, you can create a never-ending, ever-beginning circle of Reiki. To do this, sit or stand in a circle and lay your hands on the shoulders or waist of the person to your left. Now start to let Reiki flow. The effect will be more pleasant if the group is quiet and united.

This is a very beautiful and effective way of activating and putting Reiki energy to use within a whole group. This wonderful experience of giving and receiving will promote the feeling of solidarity within a group and increase its harmony.

Should a lot of practitioners be present, the circle can be extended into a spiral**, combining the energy of Reiki with the power contained in this symbol.

With time, more and more people will start to rediscover the ancient symbols of old, and awaken them to new life. Be among the first to do so.

---

*   "Man and his Symbols," by C.G. Jung, Aldus Books Ltd., London, 1964
** "The Mystic Spiral," by Jill Purce, Thanes Hudson, N. Y., 1985

Chapter 17

Help for the Dying

> *"He who fears death has lost his life."*
> Johann Gottfried Seume (Apocrypha)

All things which exist in our universe are bound by the laws of life and death. Wherever we look, we see life moving in rhythms and cyles of rest and activity. When an old form "rests" or disappears, a new one, similar to it or modified and improved in form, makes an appearance. This phenomenon is to be found everywhere, ranging from truly cosmic dimensions (a new sector of scientific investigation) to the "wave crests" and "troughs" which occur in the vibrations contained in all matter. This incessant coming and going can also be observed in our most immediate surroundings. When a blossom develops, the bud dies, when the fruit develops, the blossom dies. when a new plant develops, the fruit dies. A new day follows each night, and spring follows the stillness of winter with a fresh surge of life each year.

And yet we human beings believe in the existence of death, final and irrevocable. There is a fundamental law of physics which states that energy is never be lost but takes on another form instead. This law can easily be applied to matter, too. What is the case, however, with spirit and consciousness, those things which give the body life? Do they not consist of a more powerful form of energy than matter? To know the answer we need only compare a dead body with one that is alive. What happens then to the energy of life when a body dies?

Nearly all the old cultures and wise teachings talk of the immortality of the soul and that consciousness outlives physical death. According to these teachings, the physical body is merely the mortal vessel of the spirit and soul, an instrument which enables them to live on this planet. This handed-down form of knowledge has become subject to modern scientific investigation in a number of cases. Sir John Eccles, Nobel Prize winner of 1963, astounded his audience at the Dusseldorf World Congress of Philosophy in

1978 by stating that consciousness was fundamentally independent and that, since it could not be traced back to any kind of organic substance or function, it should be regarded as existing apart from the central nervous system. Moreover, although the spirit interrelated with the neoronic mechanisms of the brain, it was completely autonomous of them at the same time.

The French physicist, Jean E. Charon, who made himself a name with his research work into the field of elementary particles, describes in his *"L'Esprit, cet inconnu"* that his work led him to the conclusion that there had to be a time-space continuum of the spirit in correspondance to Einstein's time-space continuum of matter, a fact that presupposes a double-sidedness to all dimensions.

"According to their physical definition, spirit-laden particles are stable, which makes their life-span ... identical to that of the universe. This leads us to the conclusion that all the information invested in the course of a human life into these particles (of which our bodies consist) will continue to exist after death for all eternity."

If the spirit is something which exists independently of the body, death will be nothing other than a transition to another form of being and dimension which only the eyes of the soul can see. This "other dimension" has been described in great detail by many serious scientists, who depict it as being a subtle or spiritual world consisting of many different planes which pervade the visible, material world and complement it at the same time. These planes are also to be found in the spiritual soul of man, depending on his state of development and consciousness, and can incarnate into physical form in order to develop further. (Please see the literature below for further details.**)

However, man fears death as though it were the worst possible thing that could happen to him. As the German author and parapsychologist, Thorwald Dethlefsen says:

"Through a materialistic view of life, man's natural understanding of death as being a rhythmically occurring transition into another plane of being has been increasingly replaced by the belief that "it is all over" when you die. This results in a desparate clinging to life and a frantic

* "L' Esprit, cet inconnu," by Jean E. Charon, Editions Albin Michel, Paris, 1977.
** "Death — The Final Stage of Growth," by Elisabeth Kübler-Ross, Prentice Fall Inc., New Jersey, 1975, Eaglewood-Cliffs, New Jersey, U.S.A.

fear of the unknown to come. Usually we do not admit our fear of death to ourselves and project it onto others. When someone dies, we are reminded not only of our own dreaded death but also of the threat this means to us."

The subject of death has become taboo, something we don't talk about or like to talk about, preferring at best to pass over it in silence. The way we treat the dying reflects this attitude. Doctors try to prolong life at all costs, and we ourselves become either helpless or ill at ease when faced with someone on their deathbed.

In our day and age, Dr. Elisabeth Kübler-Ross, is well-known for her work with the dying, she has begun pleading that the dying should be treated in a manner befitting human beings and commensurate with the fundamental meaning and deeply-moving experience of dying. She says:

"The moment of transition is a natural and painless process for the dying person and is usually experienced as being something wonderful. This has been observed time and time again. The dying can teach us the point of living... Don't let those close to you die in the cold, functional atmosphere of a hospital. Bring them home, wherever possible... If only we could learn to regard death in a new way, to incorporate it into our lives and see it as an expected friend and not as a feared stranger, we would be able to live our lives with new meaning."*

If ever you happen to "accompany" someone making his transition from this world to a new level of existence, it could become a wonderful and deeply-moving experience for you, because when the soul begins to detach itself from the body, the dying freqently become more and more aware of their inner being. Thanks to modern thanatology (an area of research dealing with the process of dying and death), which is based in part on the reports of people who were brought back to life, we know more about the experiences involved in the process of dying today. Usually, the dying see a bright light and experience a feeling of peace and freedom, accompanied by a deep sense of security. Frequently they also see luminous beings who seem to be waiting for them. We find a very similar description of this at the end of Schiller's work "The Maid of Orleans," where he writes:

---

* "Questions and Answers on Death and Dying," by Elisabeth Kuebler-Ross, The MacMillan Company, New York and London

"What happens to me? Gentle clouds lift me —
my heavy armour turns to angel's dress.
Upwards — upwards — I leave the earth behind.
Short is the pain and eternal the joy."

Many of the people who were brought back to life after having laid in a state of clinical death reported that they had been able to see the doctors and the hospital surroundings while in this state. They had had the feeling of floating above their bodies and were able to hear what the doctors said about them. Frequently they were reluctant to let themselves be returned to the "prisons" of their bodies through the well-meant efforts of the doctors**.

In this context it is interesting to mention the so-called Delpasse Experiment, in which Dr. Grey-Walter, an English neurologist, trained people likely to die shortly (due to an illness) to consciously produce certain brain waves, in accordance with the bio-feedback technique. These brain waves were then intensifed by electrodes placed on the patients' heads to such an extent that the waves were capable of switching on a monitor and making an interesting picture appear. Later, when the patients actually died, memory impulses in the brain became active of their own accord and and switched the monitor on. This took place long after all the activities of the brain had ceased to function and in each case, none of the patients could be resuscitated. This experiment indicates that conscious processes can survive death.

In many cultures, death used to be and still is celebrated as being a joyful occurrence (much as we celebrate birth), since it is regarded as being a release from the limitations of earthly existence. As King Solomon said in the Bible:

"The day of death is better than the day of birth"
Ecclesiastes 7, Verse 1

In these cultures the dying were often provided with instructions for their journey as well as the assistance of a person who would accompany them through the process of dying with love and understanding.

Here Reiki can provide us with gentle but effective means for supporting and helping our loved ones and friends, our pets and, one day, ourselves, to pass through this time of transition to a new state of being. Reiki will help the dying person to adjust inwardly and prepare himself for this transition

---

* "Recollections of Death" by Dr. Michael Sabom, Harper and Row Publishing House, New York, 1962

while strengthening the bond to his inner Self, so that the body can be left without a struggle. If the person dying is ill and feels pain, he can be given additional Reiki energy where needed. Treating the Heart Chakra will help him take leave of this life in harmony and open him up for what is to come. If you take the patient's head into your hands and give him the mental treatment as well, death will become an experience of liberation and fulfillment. If the person dying is unconscious, do not think that he is no longer able to benefit from the Reiki energy you are giving him. As Dr. Kübler-Ross says:

> *"Above all, do not think that the dying person can no longer feel your love and affection. A dying person can feel everything, even when he is in a state of coma."*

If your work involves frequent contact with the dying, as would be the case in the intensive-care ward of hospital or in an old-people's home, Reiki will become an indispensable form of help for both yourself and for the people in your care.

It is also a way of staying in contact with life, even and especially in situations where we are confronted with death. Furthermore, Reiki will let us experience a sense of union with the dying person which will transcend all separation.

Chapter 18

Treating Animals with Reiki

Since Reiki consists of the same universal life energy which makes flowers grow, birds fly and the the world go round, the fact that it will heal the ailments of all kinds of animals too will not be astonishing. Moreover, the fact that animals can be healed with Reiki proves its effectivity, because an animal will not be cured by a psychological trick, hypnosis or by belief alone. In this respect, we must think of the situation of acupuncture in West Germany, where a great step forward was made when a few experienced practitioners began to apply it successfully to horses, dogs and cows. At last it was posible to refute the theory that acupuncture only worked because the patients were psychologically influenced in its favor.

Of course, Reiki is not dependent on any kind of scientific recognition. After all, what would have become of creation if its existence had depended on frequently-changing scientific opinion. The whole immeasurable variety of the universe existed long before science confirmed it. Furthermore, since the time when people began to analyze structures and formulate theorems and tenets, certain phenomena have received scientific confirmation while others have not. In many of these cases, it would frequently be more correct to say that the laws inherent in one kind of phenomena have been detected while they have not been in others. All these considerations are of no concern to the animals we treat. The successes to be experienced in the treatment of animals with Reiki amounts to an objective confirmation of its effectiveness and may one day help awaken the interest of science in this amazing method of healing.

Although we do not know what animals experience when we treat them with Reiki, we do notice that they tend to get quieter. Something in them seems to let go and relax. The principles of treatment will always be the same, whether you are a vet treating a circus elephant or a mother taking care of a frog found by her children. You will soon notice that Reiki literally *flows* into animals, just as it does with people.

When we treat domestic animals, such as horses, cows, pigs, cats and dogs, we lay our hands behind their ears at the point where dogs like to be stroked, for example. After that, we treat the rest of the body systematically or we let our hands remain at places where the animal seems to feel pain or where it is ill. It's as easy as that, the procedure for treating animals not differing from that for treating people. In both cases, we always let ourselves be guided by our inner feeling and let our hands linger whenever it seems necessary. In the case of small animals such as mice, hamsters, guinea pigs and birds it is best to cup them comfortably in your hands, where they will soon become noticeably quieter. Do not be worried if the heartbeat is very rapid, it is naturally swifter than that of human beings. Reiki can also be given to an animal when it is asleep, but be sure to hold your hand at a slight distance above it so that it is not disturbed.

If you want to treat fish, take the aquarium between your hands and let Reiki energy flow for 15 to 20 minutes. You have to use your imagination in the case of animals such as penguins, snakes and butterflies. If a giraffe gets earache for example, you can take a ladder, lean it against a tree and wait until the giraffe gets hungry. Of course, absentee treatment would be much easier in this case, but it wouldn't be as adventurous.

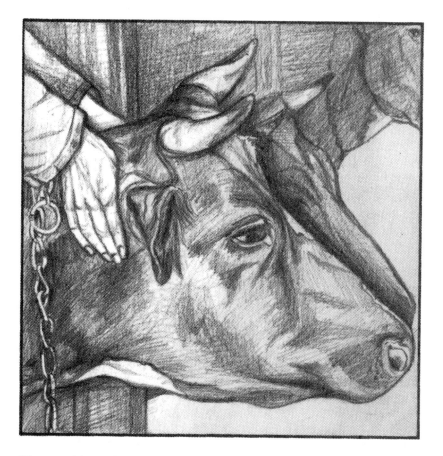

We were able to observe the effect of Reiki on animals at close hand while we were writing this chapter. We were sitting in the sun in a little pine clearing near our mountain lodge when a herd of ten young cows made an appearance. They were obviously curious and each one had to smell us and, if possible, lick us, too. They had returned to their grazing when one of them caught our attention. It was thinner than the rest and had a kind of cough. Shalila immediately began an absentee treratment of it at a distance of about three feet, whereupon the cow sank its head, half-closed its eyes and stood quietly while the other cows went on busily grazing. When the treatment came to an end, the cow livened up again and went back to cropping

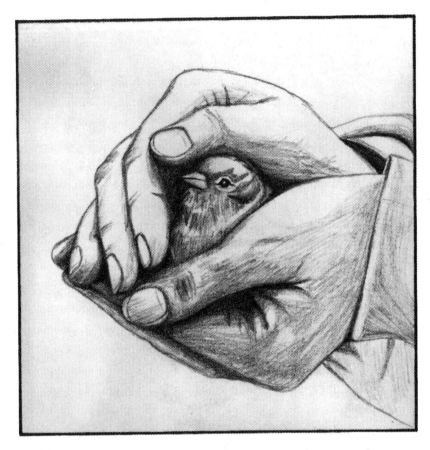

the grass. Unfortunately, we didn't see this herd of cows again, so we couldn't check the result of Shalila's treatment.

This demonstrates clearly that animals can be treated with the absentee method (as well as the mental technique). Both methods will often be the easiest ways of treating animals that are too big or too small, too frightened or simply too dangerous to be treated directly.

Compared to other animals, cats tend to react to Reiki treatment differently. The position behind the ears usually becomes unpleasant for them after a short while and they become restless. Snakes and bees also react this way and the same is probably true of wasps, hornets and ants, which all seem to form an exception in the animal kingdom.

With time you will surely build up your own store of experience in the treatment of animals with Reiki.

Chapter 19

Plants enjoy Reiki too

Perhaps you have once experienced a wonderful state of consciousness where you were closely united to the whole of creation. On this level, everything which usually separated you from the rest of life disappeared and you became part of everything around you and everything around you

became part of your own eternal being. In the Upanishads, this state is described as being "I am that, you are that, everything is that." C.G. Jung called it the collective unconscious and Jesus was referring to it when he said "I and my Father are one." (John 10:30)

Whoever has experienced this inspired state of unity will know that the difference separating us from our so-called surroundings is very slight indeed. This also applies to the universal energy of life, which manifests itself in the different forms of man and beast, plant and mineral. All these forms are but expressions of different stages of development in the game of life.

Knowing this, it is not difficult to understand why not only humans and animals like being given Reiki, but why flowers, trees shrubs and seeds enjoy it, too. When we give Reiki, we pass on a concentrated form of the same life energy which flows through all of us and keeps us alive.

When you start giving Reiki to plants, you will soon be impressed by the positive results, such as strong, healthy growth and, profusion of blossoms. A simple test will demonstrate this well. Take two plants of the same kind and stand them slightly apart in identical conditions. Treat one of the plants with Reiki daily. If you compare the plants after a period of time you will notice a considerable difference. The same test can be applied to seeds, cut flowers, trees and bushes. Please keep in mind, however, that positive reactions will take time to develop in slow-growing species. Generally speaking, plants seem to take to Reiki just like human beings and will often live longer than average as a result.

In order to enrich seeds with Reiki, hold your hands a few inches above them, as if you were blessing them. You can also put the seeds into your left hand and give them Reiki with your right. In this case, you also hold your hand a few inches above them for a few minutes. Seedlings already growing in the earth can be treated where they stand by holding your hand above them until they have received enough Reiki.

Cut flowers are treated by taking the vase between your hands and letting the Reiki energy flow through it. This can be done daily with no fear of overdosing, because plants only take as much as they need.

Potted plants are best treated via the roots, with the pot held between your hands as a vase of flowers. At a Reiki meeting an acquaintance once told us how she treated a sick plant. She gave it Reiki a few times but could not feel the familiar "flowing" feeling. It was as if the plant had closed up and was not able to take in the energy. So the girl started talking to her plant, telling it how she intended to treat it, as if it were a patient. The next time she treated it, the plant opened up and the energy was able to flow through to it again.

It would certainly be no mistake for any of us to give our plants more conscious attention and to think of them in a loving way.

Trees can be given Reiki, too. Since they take it in through their trunks you can hug them if you want to. They generally prefer a lengthier dose of treatment, but, here again, let yourself be guided by your inner feeling. When we treat a tree it always leaves us feeling very balanced and harmonious.

Sometimes we have transferred Reiki as a group to whole woods of weakened and dying trees. The positive impulses involved probably help the trees more than being afraid and expecting the worst to happen, because our thoughts and feelings can take on very concrete form on the physical plane. Shrubs can also be treated by closing them in your arms, while another way of giving your plants Reiki would be to enrich their water.

If you have attained Second Degree Reiki, you will also be able to make use

of absentee healing and the mental method on plants with success. The only practicable way of treating whole woods at once, for example, is via the absentee method.

There is surely a plane of existence where plants are able to express their gratitude. Be aware of this and open yourself up to it. Even on this plane there can be an "exchange of energy."

---

* Translator's note: German woods are reacting to the effects of acid rain at an alarming rate. Similar reactions are also found in the United States, particularly in the case of the redwoods, as American scientists have found out recently.

Chapter 20

Further Uses for Reiki

So far we have discussed treating people, animals and plants with Reiki. However, it can also be put to a variety of other uses, a few of which we would like to describe here.

Although Reiki is generally used for situations where there is a deficiency or lack of harmony, it can also be used to enrich things with additional life

energy, such as food, medicine, plasters, bandages, clothes and shoes, as well as pieces of jewelry and gems that mean a lot to you.

You can turn a present into a double gift by treating it with Reiki beforehand and it can be sent in your letters, too. If your car won't start in winter, try treating it with Reiki first, putting your hands around the battery for a few minutes before starting up the engine again. Some friends of ours have carried out this method with success quite often and, if someone is with you, you can get them to start the engine while you are still "treating" the battery.

If you are in possession of Second Degree Reiki, you can clear every room of negative vibrations and replace them with harmonious, life-giving ones instead. This is particularly useful in hotels and train compartments, but you may also want to make use of this possibility in your home and car, too. You will feel much better for it afterwards.

With a little thought, you will discover more ways of putting Reiki to use in everyday life. Since Reiki flows all the more strongly the more often it is used, do not hesitate to try it out in such unusual ways.

Chapter 21

Can Reiki be Combined with Other Forms of Treatment?

Some of the people who go to Reiki seminars already know a whole variety of therapy systems, and so the question is frequently posed whether Reiki can be used in combination with this or that method. Again, our patients often ask us whether Reiki will be compatible with the medicine they are taking or another form of treatment they are presently undergoing.

According to modern-day findings, Reiki will both support and increase the effectiveness of almost every kind of medication and treatment presently known. It can be used in combination with surgery as well as all other kinds of treatment, including physiotherapy. This is made possible by the fact that Reiki will detoxify the body and cleanse and harmonize it, as well as supporting biological healing processes in a holistic manner.

However, there is one exception to this rule. Reiki should never be given during an operation because the narcosis could start to work in an unexpected way. Instead, it can be given beforehand or afterwards. Reiki will also speed up the healing of a broken bone but, here again, it is better to wait until the bone has been set before applying Reiki.

At this point, we would like to emphasize that Reiki is not a substitute for every other kind of medication and treatment. However, it will complement and support the biological healing processes that are set in motion by these methods.

Many doctors, psychologists and natural health practitioners who combine Reiki with other forms of treatment have achieved good results. Bodo, for example, has been able to combine Reiki with *massage, reflex zone therapy, breathing therapy, Touch for Health, Polarity, Pre-natal Therapy* and many others, including *the injection of procaine into scar tissue.* Other practitioners we know of use Reiki with *acupuncture, acupressure, the massage of acupressure points, shiatsu, kitsu, tai-ki, an-no, do-in, E.A.S., jin shin, jiutsu, chiropractics, color therapy, Bach flower remedies, homeopathy, aroma therapy, Ayurveda, fasting* and various forms of *psychotherapy.* Other therapists and teachers are known to combine Reiki with *meditation, bio-energetics* and *autogeneous training* as well as other methods. Reiki can also be transferred to the patient with the injection fluid when he is getting an injection.

For all these reasons, Reiki is especially helpful for all people involved in healing in the broadest sense, for it will complement almost every kind of treatment we know of in a wonderful and natural way. In this sense, Reiki can be compared to clean fresh air, which will help almost every kind of patient to get better and which is indeed one of the basic requirements for a healthy life. In the final analysis, Reiki will attune all the levels of a person in such a way that a holistic, whole-istic development will take place.

It may happen that Reiki will be laughed at, but this will generally be the result of prejudice and ignorance. We all tend to regard the new and unusual with scepticism at first — the result of our Western upbringing, which teaches us to regard the world in a rational way. Apparently, this was no different in Schopenhauer's time:

> *"Before a problem achieves recognition as such,*
> *It has to go through three stages:*
> *In the first one it is laughed at,*
> *During the second it will be fought against;*
> *Until, in the third, it is accepted as being self- evident."*

In West Germany, the costs of hospitalization have increased to such an extent that they are hardly financeable. In such a case, it would be worth while to experiment using Reiki in hospitals. One practitioner could be allotted to every 10-15 patients and an evaluation of the statistics regarding the course of illness and length of stay might prove to be very interesting. Reiki could definitely be made use of in psychiatric wards and children's hospitals as well as in birth preparation courses and during convalescence. In this respect, West Germany is still one step behind the United States, where Reiki is a recognized supplementary form of treatment taught to doctors, nurses and psychologists.

This proves that a change in thought is taking place. There is a noticeable shift towards living out one's spirituality and doing things in a natural way, and more and more people are adopting a more holistic approach to life which they are also putting into practice.

We are living in a time of radical change and have reached the "turning point" of Fritjof Capra. Ferguson's "gentle conspirators" may still be treading softly, but they are gaining ground steadily.

"What would happen,
If everybody said,
"What would happen?"
And nobody went,
To take a look,
At what would happen,
If something happened."

We, therefore, feel that a method of healing like Reiki will gain more and more recognition in the future. We feel that it will slowly begin to replace those other methods of treatment which are based on the treatment of symptoms alone and which do not take into consideration that man is a totality of mind, body and soul.

Happiness

In life there is only one duty,
And that is the duty of happiness.
This is the reason for our being here,
But all our duties,
Moral codes,
And regulations,
Do not make us happy,
And so we seldom make each other happy.
If man is to be good
He can only be so
When he is happy,
When he carries harmony within,
In other words, when he loves.
This is the Teaching,
The only Teaching in the world;
The one taught by Jesus Christ
The one taught by Buddha
And taught by Hegel, too.
For each one of us, the most important thing in the world
Is his inmost being,
His soul,
His ability to love.
If this is in good order,
You can eat cake or crusts,
Wear jewels or rags,
And the world will ring in purity with the soul,
Will be good,
Will be in good order.

Taken from the literary bequest of Hermann Hesse

Chapter 22

When Reiki Doesn't Seem to Work . . .

People who frequently treat with Reiki will probably notice that the results they have been expecting do not always occur. What could be the reason for this?

In this chapter, we would like to mention some of the factors involved in this and hope that the following information will help you judge the reactions made by your patients, whether in the treatment room or otherwise.

One of the most frequent reasons for apparent failure will be the fact that we had been expecting a certain kind of effect to occur, and then the natural law according to which Reiki functions brought about something else. In this case, although our expectations have not been fulfilled, it may well be that something which is not immediately apparent has taken place within the patient. After all, not everyone likes to talk about his inner life and important changes often start to take place on this level. Frequently, the patient himself has no clear idea of what has been going on within him, and it may take weeks or even months before the effects of such a treatment become clear.

Therefore, do not be disappointed if your expectations are not fulfilled immediately. With Reiki, nothing is to be achieved by pure willpower. Our egos have to take second place instead, which is not bad for our development. As Reiki channels, we do not do the healing ourselves but are simply neutral observers and witnesses of events. For this reason, we should never disapprove of a patient's symptoms. It is not our task to fight against an illness but to pass on Reiki energy and await the results, which will always be the best ones possible.

However, there are some interesting reasons why Reiki sometimes fails to work. For example, we have experienced again and again that, although patients come for treatment, the willingness to be healed is simply an alibi. In their innermost beings such patients, consciously or unconsciously, do not want to be made healthy again. On the contrary, they cling to their illnesses, which are obviously advantageous to them in some way. There was once a housewife, for example, who only got the support and affection of her family when she was ill. This was probably the only way she had. When this kind of experience is deeply rooted, the patient will probably have an inner resistance to any kind of treatment that could help him. Of course, on the outside it will look as if he has done everything he could to become healthy again; no stone has been left unturned, and even your "new, exotic" method has been given a try.

You will discover a similar phenomenon in the case of children, but not generally to such a marked degree. When a child is ill, it is taken care of and generally shown a lot of love and sympathy. It won't have to go to school, may get lots of visitors and presents, and everyone will be generally nice to him or her. When such a child has balanced out what it had been previously lacking, it will then, but only then, find it easy to become healthy again. This mechanism is generally an unconscious one, and we should not get cross when a child seems to be making use of it, for it is often the only way children have of bringing things into balance again.

Don't we feel this way, too, sometimes. For weeks or months we overdo things and then, when we can no longer go on, we become ill, gaining the peace and quiet we had not been granting ourselves as well as the care and attention of our loved ones, which we had not been been getting, in a way which is generally accepted. After all, a sick person is sympathised with, for it is not his fault for getting ill at exactly that moment in time. And once he gets better, everything will seem rosy again. Seen from this point of view, getting ill was actually very sensible.

There are further reasons for Reiki apparently failing to have the desired effect. It once happened to Bodo that a woman did not return after she had been treated for the first time, which puzzled him very much. He then found out from her sister that she had experienced Reiki as being something strange and dubious. We do not know why she reacted in this way, but we do know that there are people who react better on a more material level. These are generally people who have never encountered spiritual things before and who prefer something a little more "solid" than Reiki. In such a case, it is best to respect the patient's wishes and treat him or her respectively. Since each one of us is at a different stage of development, we probably need respective methods of treatment.

For this reason, never try to persuade someone to let himself be treated with Reiki. Instead, simply tell him what Reiki is and how it works and leave the decision up to him. This will generally lead to satisfactory treatment.

Another reason for Reiki apparently failing to work might be that the person involved has not yet learned the "lesson" taught by the illness and that he therefore has to go on being ill for a little while. On the other hand, illness may prevent a person from repeatedly breaking laws of nature and doing damage to himself, in which case Reiki treatment could well open up such a patient's eyes to the inner causes of his condition. In this case, the patient suddenly becomes aware of why he or she is ill and starts to change things on an inner and outer level. Then there is the case of patients who have to pay a *karmic debt* before they can be healed, and here again Reiki will be of help. Other patients may need to be cured by another practitioner than yourself, also for karmic reasons, but this does not happen very often. There is also the kind of patient who finds Reiki too simple. Such patients are afraid that people will think they hadn't really been ill if they could be cured so easily. Anything under three weeks in hospital is unacceptable. What can you say to that?

A last category of "problem patients" are those who come for treatment in order to prove to you and themselves that a method like Reiki cannot possibly have any effect whatsoever. They lie on the treatment table full of tension and scepticism, resisting every flow of energy and every kind of pleasant feeling and fighting the possibility of inner change occurring and harmony setting in. Some of them will manage to remain in the right to the end.

"Someone who isn't convinced of something himself won't be convinced about it by you either."

Plato

Therefore, when someone comes to you for treatment, provide him with information and offer him the possibility of treatment but do not press it on him. Each person has his own free will, and we should respect this.

However, these things do not occur very often and their existence should not prevent us from approaching each new case in an unbiased way. Our reason for describing them here is simply to help you deal with them should they come about.

We are convinced that you will experience very wonderful cures with Reiki, although the way they come about will sometimes surprise you. Simply remain open for what is to occur.

Chapter 23

Some Thoughts Regarding the Legal Situation and "Energy Exchange"

It is a beautiful and natural wish to want to practice Reiki on a broad basis and to treat as many people as possible, and we wish all people doing so much success. However, there are certain regulations which govern the practice of medical treatment and these differ from country to country.

If you are a doctor, you will obviously be able to apply Reiki whenever you deem it necessary, no matter the country you practise in. Your main hurdle will be the one of time, for doctors generally plan their appointments very tightly and a Reiki treatment requires a fair amount. Of course, you can treat problematical areas quickly once in a while, but generally full length sessions will be preferrable. A solution in this case would be to employ one or more Reiki practitioners in your practice or to collaborate with some on a free-lance basis.

It is advisable for doctors practising Reiki to inform their patients beforehand about the kind of treatment Reiki is and the way it works, to avoid getting surprised reactions. An information sheet can also be prepared for the patient to read beforehand.

Apart from doctors, there are further professional groups involved to a certain extent in the "healing or alleviation of human illness for gain," including in some countries pedicurists, chiropodists, podiatrists, gymnastic teachers, masseurs, ambulance and first-aid professionals, medical assistants, midwives, nurses, Gestalt therapists, meditation teachers, breathing therapists, yoga teachers, health advisers and drug counsellors. Even qualified cosmeticians are allowed to work with laser beams and electrotherapy devices these days. Of course, the legal regulations concerning some of these professions differ from country to country and we therefore advise you to take a close look at what you are allowed and not allowed to do before carrying out Reiki as part of your work. *The following is of absolute importance, however, you should never make a diagnosis or make use of the word: you should not undertake any kind of action that goes*

beneath the surface of the skin and, of course, you should not prescribe any
kind of medication or advise your patient to discontinue taking any. What is
possible, however, and surely not liable to punishment under any kind of
medical legislation, is to let Reiki flow while carrying out your regular professional work.

We have heard objections however concerning absentee treatment, for many
people think that healing over a distance is absolutely impossible and that
absentee treatment could be regarded as fraud from a legal point of view.
However, absentee treatment is no different from the direct method, for the
practitioner places himself at disposal as a channel for the healing energies
to flow through in both cases and, therefore, we are of the opinion that the
legal situation concerning absentee treatment is no different than the direct
one. Since the distance involved cannot be regarded as a fact liable to punish-

ment, a practitioner can only be accused of fraud if fixed fees are charged. Should you be dependent on the income earned in this way, we advise you to let the patient pay whatever he feels fit or to accept payment in the form of a donation.

We now come to the situation of the layman who does not practice Reiki as a means of earning a living. No country in the world has regulations forbidding mothers the right to lay their hands on their children. And no one will object to your touching your husband or wife or friends either. However, when you treat people outside your closest circle of friends, do not publicly advertise the fact that Reiki is a healing method, since someone could come to the conclusion that you are illegally running a medical practice. In this case it is better not to make use of the term "patient"; either "client," "recipient" or "friend" will do just as well.

We know of a couple who teach yoga, rebirthing and reincarnation therapy and who have begun to practice Reiki, too. They call Reiki a "relaxation technique" and are able to carry it out without coming into conflict with the law. In terms of legal jurisdiction, the term "relaxation technique" is a good one, since the patient does indeed experience a strong sense of relaxation, and relaxation is conducive to a state of health, whether intentionally or not. The patient is also not touched directly, since he remains clothed during treatment. In case of doubt, please check the legal situation in your own country. Each person is responsible for himself in this respect, and each one of us must decide for himself what he may or may not do.

Some countries are often very generous in their legal attitude towards alternative or spiritual methods of healing. For example, in Great Britain patients can now request spirit healing in over 2,000 clinics. The "Spiritualist Association of Great Britain" (SAGB) led by Tom Johanson, is the largest one of its kind in the world.

Furthermore, there is also a National Federation of Spirit Healers" (NFSH) in England, led by Diana Craig. Other countries may also have similar organizations. In case of need, it might be worth while to make enquiries. If there are no such organizations in your country, consider founding one to support your interests and help you in all affairs connected with healing.

In an English clinic where "spiritual healing" is practised in addition to other methods, a discerning senior physician once made a very apt remark about the lack of recognition granted to spiritual healing. He said, "On the one hand, we have the right to get ill in every imaginable way, but on the other we don't have the right to be cured in every imaginable way. Or do we indeed?"

We have never come across any cases of people coming into conflict with the law because of Reiki. However, should you for any reason ever happen to have to go to prison, remember you can make good use of your time doing Reiki or a form of meditation. Let your time "behind bars" become one of stillness and use it to go into yourself. If you are a Reiki channel, you will be able to treat yourself and your fellow-prisoners as well as doing much good with the absentee method. Bodo once had to "do time" in an East German prison for political reasons, but as he had learned a new form of meditation beforehand, he was able to practise it with positive results during his stay.

If Fate passes you a lemon,
make lemonade out of it!
Maharishi Mahesh Yogi

With regards to payment, assuming you require it, your patients will generally have to pay for Reiki treatment themselves, unless it is covered by their medical insurance. However, we would like to recommend "exchanging energy," as it is called in Findhorn, as a legitimate means of paying for Reiki. Energy does not always have to be in the form of money, although money is recognized as being such in our society. Instead, if someone is willing to darn all your socks, this could be an acceptable means of payment to you. This way, you might even find yourself being provided with healthy fruit and vegetables from the nice people living on the organically-run farm nearby. In our experience, this kind of energy exchange is a very straightforward one and often very pleasurable too.

While we were staying in Thailand in a very poor and remote district, we treated some natives who came to us from a nearby village and who brought fruit and nuts, hard-boiled eggs and beautiful shells with them in return for treatment. One woman however brought nothing, and, since she was very poor and owned nothing, she asked us whether she could pray for us instead. This was the most valuable and precious offering she had to make and of course we accepted gratefully. She was then able to accept treatment in the consciousness of being able to do something good for us in return. It is never a mistake to let go of rigid forms and open ourselves up to natural ones instead, for in this way we can develop many new means of communication with each other.

Why is an exchange of energy necessary at all? In answer, we would like to relate an incident from the days of Dr. Hayashi's Reiki Clinic in Tokyo. Once, a very rich but very ill lady came to the Clinic for treatment and her case soon proved to be very problematic, since treatment did not seem to be having any effect. Apparently, she was unable to take on Reiki energy for some reason.

"If you pour pieces of gold into a hand which is full of stones, the gold will fall off. You will first of all have to give up something of yourself in order to make room for something new."

The lady in question was paying the usual fees, but the amount involved meant very little to her. Then someone got the idea to train her to become a Reiki channel herself and have her treat other patients so that an exchange of energy could take place. Much to the surprise of her practitioner, she agreed to the idea. No sooner had she started treating other people, than her own treatment began to take effect and she began to get better. Because the cycle of energy had been closed, she was able to receive Reiki herself.

This principle of give-and-take is applicable in all areas of our lives. There are plenty of resources available but they often don't flow sufficiently. If we overly cling to what we own while not being prepared to take on the new, the flow will begin to slacken and falter. This does not only happen on the material level but also on emotional and spiritual ones. In the long run, taking love or knowledge or anything else without giving in return will function as little as breathing in without breathing out. Giving and taking should always be in balance.

It is not always easy to assess the value of Reiki treatment in terms of money, but as a a rough guideline we feel that a Reiki session is comparable to a skilled craftsman's working hour. Depending on whether you make your living with Reiki, or whether you simply treat every now and then, you do not necessarily have to tie yourself down to a certain price. In the latter case, you may be satisfied with other methods of "payment."

Chapter 24

Tips for Reiki Practice

We would now like to give you a few hints and suggestions on how to create an optimal environment for giving Reiki. Of course, Reiki can be given anywhere. Whether on a train, in a bus or a plane, on the beach or in the woods, no special surroundings will be necessary. All the same, our suggestions may help you to create an environment for both yourself and your patient to feel comfortable in, and maybe they will also help your work to become easier and more enjoyable. We hope you find some suggestions that appeal to you.

All people are influenced by surroundings to a certain extent. For this reason, it is a good idea to arrange the area where you give Reiki in such a way that it reflects the love, peace and harmony Reiki conveys. Outer chaos will hardly contribute towards a sense of inner harmony.

First of all, it is important to make sure that you will not be disturbed while you are treating. A person who is in a deep state of relaxation will be shocked out of it very abruptly by a barking dog, a ringing telephone, or someone looking in for your advice. Therefore, always remove the receiver from the telephone and hang up a "Do not disturb — Reiki" sign on your door when you are treating. You should never treat to the sound of radio or television either, unless you are doing a "quickie" on the spur of the moment.

It is also important to plan enough time for treatment. Generally speaking, an hour will be sufficient. It will also be very important to have a short introductory conversation beforehand between only yourself and your patient, if possible, in which case you will find a confidential atmosphere very helpful. Exchange a few friendly words once treatment is over — some patients will be positively overflowing with what they have just experienced. Others, however, will be needing a little peace and quiet and should be allowed to remain lying down for a little while if they want to. This time of stillness is often very important, and for this reason some practitioners have two separate treatment rooms.

And now a few words about the practioner himself, who should be calm and composed during treatment. Meditation or autogeneous training, etc. will often prove to be very helpful in this respect. The practitioner should make sure that he doesn't smell of garlic, tobacco or a very strong perfume because sensitive patients could react defensively to such smells and a defensive reaction is not particularly conducive to relaxation. Since the practitioner works with his hands, he should always wash them beforehand and, of course, no one should smoke during treatment.

If you are able to furnish your place of treatment yourself, this is a wonderful opportunity, but of course this will depend on whether you give Reiki in a practice or whether you treat only your family and friends. Whatever the case, try to make your place of treatment somewhere very special, a place where you like to be and where you feel apart from the affairs of everyday life. With very few means, such as some beautiful plants or flowers, a few

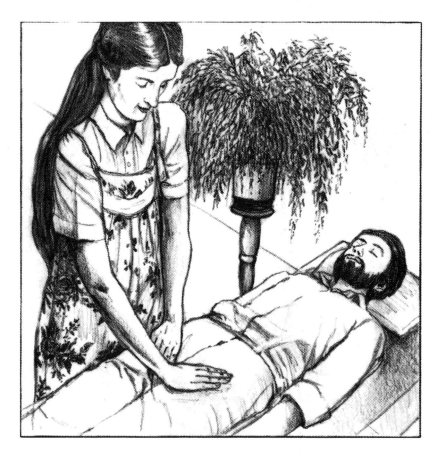

stones and shells and a good picture, you will be able to create surroundings which will radiate a feeling of peace and harmony. A carpet or flooring made of natural materials will also be a big help. Choose a subdued means of lighting and avoid neon tubes or spotlights, which would bathe the patient in a flood of direct light. A certain amount of tidiness and cleanliness in this area will also contribute to a sense of inner order. The room should not be cooler than 21 ° C, since a lying person easily gets cold at temperatures below this level. If the room is well aired, you can scent it slightly with incense sticks or, preferably, perfume oils. Make sure your incense sticks are not too intensive.

If you are in a position to play quiet, relaxing music in the background, this will create optimal conditions for treatment. Try to use a cassette-recorder with an auto-reverse function to avoid the disturbing "click" that occurs when the cassette comes to an end. You also won't have to get up and turn the cassette over either. "Majesty" and "Angel Love" by Aeoliah is the most optimal therapy music we know of at the moment, but we also like Steven Halpern, Paul Horn, Kitaro, Daniel Kobialka as well as "Angelic Music" and other pieces by Iasos. The natural sounds of a stream, the woods or the sea are also very suitable, as is classical music by Bach, Mozart, Handel, Vivaldi and Pachelbel, which should be kept at a very low volume. Since there are very few cassettes or records which are entirely suitable for playing to Reiki treatment, we often tape our own. Always make sure that the music you are playing is suitable for the patient lying on your couch. After all, it is the patient above all who should be made comfortable.

The best kind of background music would be a stream flowing past your treatment room. We once treated in an old water-mill and, another time, next to a waterfall, and the sound of moving water was very harmonious. A wind harp or reed pipes also sound beautiful and natural. Sounds which are experienced as being pleasant always have a soothing effect; moreover, they reduce the effect made by disturbing ones. The book, "The Live Energy of Music," by Dr. John Diamond is very informative in this respect.

If you know a good *dowser* you could have him investigate the treatment couch (and also your bed) to find out whether they stand above geopathic fields of interference (such as crossing water veins). If this is the case, you can either move the treatment couch or else neutralize the interference yourself by putting a pot of silica sand (obtainable in glass factories) under the couch and spreading a jute fiber sheet over it, beneath any other layers. (You should put the silica sand in the sun at least once a year to neutralize it.) An ionizer, which produces negatively-charged oxygen ions, is advisable for all working and treatment rooms. You will also need fresh running water to wash your hands as well as a toilet with a mirror.

And now we come to an important point. Since the patient lies during treatment, you will need something for him to lie on which is suitable for both the patient and yourself. On the one hand, the patient must be able to feel comfortable, while, on the other, you must be able to reach all parts of his body without straining your back and neck muscles.

Some practitioners like to work sitting on the edge of a mattress, while others wouldn't be able to stand it for longer than five minutes. A friend of ours puts three mattresses on top of each other so they reach a height of about 20 inches, and then she treats sitting on a "knee-chair" (illustrated in chapter 23), which is an optimal means of sitting upright without a backrest. However, this method doesn't solve the problem of reaching all the parts of the patient's body in the easiest possible way.

If you do a lot of work with Reiki, you should try to discover the most optimal way of giving treatment for you, even if it means having to make an investment. After all, pleasant working conditions will increase the joy that is felt when Reiki is being given. A good solution is the one used by our Reiki Master, Brigitte Müller, who uses a wheeled office chair to roll about to the different parts of the patient's body. We also find the pendulum stool, which is illustrated in chapter 11, an interesting possibility. (The pendulum stool is constructed in such a way that it will not tip over when leaned too far.) Two or three of these stools positioned around the massage couch will save you having to carry one around with you when you move about. Of course, you can also stand to treat, but, as you will often have to lean forward, you will be placing an unnecessary strain on your spinal chord. The height the couch will depend on the practitioner in question, but should be so high that you can lay your hands on the patient comfortably without having to stoop (about 2-2 1/2 feet). If the bench isn't as high as that, you can spread your legs a bit instead of leaning over, which will make up for about 8 inches.

There are also treatment couches which can be raised up and down at the press of a button by means of an oil-hydraulic pump mechanism or with an electric lifting system. Apart from the expensive prices involved, we do not find it a good idea to be dependent on electricity, and it doesn't seem wise to position a motor beneath the patient's body either.

The couch should not be narrower than 2 feet, so that the Reiki recipient can lie with his arms comfortably next to him without having to push them under his body. Broader people also have to feel comfortable on your couch. 6-6 1/2 feet will be sufficient in length. When the patient is lying on his stomach, he will often find it very pleasant if there is an opening for his face, and if the head section can be adjusted up or down. Choose a very soft and comfortable couch, if possible; patients should let themselves be spoiled once in a while.

If you make home visits, you will need a *portable massage couch*, but you can also treat with a blanket on a kitchen table. Whatever kind of couch you choose, always use clean sheets and keep a blanket within reach. A roll of foam rubber, which can be laid under the ankles of the patient when he is lying on his stomach, will aid relaxation greatly. Some people also like to have a little pillow.

As we once mentioned, there are sometimes emotional tears during a Reiki treatment, and so it is good to keep a box of tissues at hand. We will also need them to cover up the patient's face when we treat it, for he may find having our hands on his face unpleasant. He will also be less distracted by other things. For this reason, the tissues should be soft and non-perfumed and large in size.

You will not require any oil, cream or any kind of medicine for treating with Reiki, but some practitioners keep Rescue Remedy (from Bach's Flower Remedies) at hand in case of need, for they can help to counterbalance strong feelings. However, you will very seldom need to use Rescue Remedy, if at all.

We must admit that this has become a very long list of suggestions. The main thing, of course, is the treatment itself, which can be carried out in the most primitive of conditions with equal success. All the same, we hope you have found a few ideas you would like to make use of.

Whatever your conditions of treatment are, giving Reiki is always good. As the proverb says, "As the question, so the answer."

While reading this book, you will surely have noticed how simple and natural Reiki is, and how effective and many-sided it is, too. If this has made you curious to get to know more about it, this book will have fulfilled its purpose. If you are even inspired to become a Reiki practitioner, we will be especially happy, and if you are already a practitioner, we hope that you have found some interesting ideas and tips.

Whatever the case, we wish each and every one of you the same sense of fulfillment, growth and happiness that we ourselves have been privileged to experience with this wonderful method of healing.

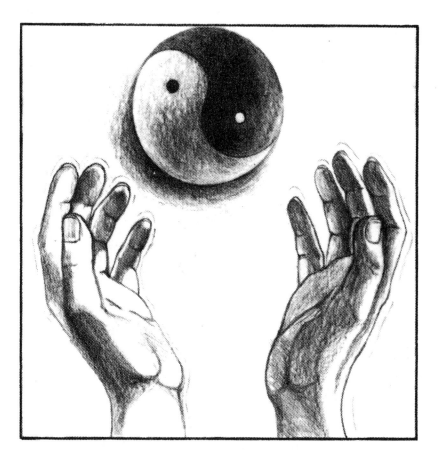

Unity

As soon as we comprehend existence as
being a complex unity
And illness as development,
Life will let us go
To wander through higher spheres
Where we will understand that growth and decay
Are but an expression of this unity.

Chapter 25

The Meaning of Illness

Again and again we are asked why pain, illness and suffering exist. Some people think illness happens by accident or that it is determined by fate, while others see it as a punishment meted out by a higher power.

Illness is regarded as being one of the greatest evils in the world and no measures are spared in finding ways of fighting and doing away with it, as evidenced by expressions like the "successful fight" the various symptoms of disease.

Quite obviously, very little is understood about the inner meaning of illness, pain and suffering. Illness is universally regarded as being one of man's great enemies which we fight against it in a battle without end, for hardly has one disease been vanquished, another rises to take its place.

This general ignorance about the meaning of illness has existed since religion (*religio* to reconnect) and the art of healing started to follow two different and independent paths, meaning that an integrated and undivided approach to the cause of suffering became lost. The division of medicine into different disciplines, such as mental and physical, has led us even farther away from the old holistic view of disease.

All the same, there have always been great spiritual men who were and and still are aware of the role played by illness in our development. As an example, we quote Dr. Edward Bach **, an English doctor who lived from 1886 to 1936:

". . . disease, though apparently so cruel, is in itself beneficient and for our good and, if rightly interpreted, ... will guide us to our essential

---

* The word *symptom* means "sign, mark", "characteristic" or "indication". A number of symptoms is also known as a " clinical picture". *Symptomatology* is the theory of the signs and characteristics of an illness.

** "Heal Thyself" by Edward Bach, C.W. Daniel Company Ltd., London, 1931 *faults. If properly treated it will be the cause of the removal of those faults and leave us better and greater than before. Suffering is a corrective to point out a lesson which by other means we have failed to grasp, and never can it be eradicated until that lesson is learnt."*

The path of truth and light is one which leads us to recognize the inner unity of life with all existence. The symptoms displayed by our illnesses point out where we have left this path. A symptom is to be regarded as a kind of information medium which helps us to recognize and integrate aspects of our being which we are either not conscious of or which we have repressed or not wanted to know about or which we have lost altogether over the passage of time. It is this non-consciousness which makes us become ill.

This approach is based on the knowledge that *"all that is visible is but an allegory",* as Goethe once put it, or in other words, that all that is visible is a manifestation of an intention or idea. In this respect, ideas and intentions seek physical matter or events which they can express themselves with. In the case of illness these will be viruses, bad eating habits etc. "Chance" encounters, accidents and other "coincidences" are also typical "Agents of Fate", as Wolfgang Döbereiner, a Munich astrologer puts it.

When Einstein's formula e = mc² proved that matter and energy are exchangeable, he came very close to this truth. In this sense, our bodies are outward signs of inward consciousness, just as a painting is the visible expression of an artist's ideas. One of Bodo's teachers, Prof. Kurt Tepperwein expressed this same idea in the following way:

"Our bodies, indeed our whole lives, are nothing other than a reflection of our spiritual situation, for it is the spirit which forms the body and determines our fate."

This means that in the outer and visible aspects of our in other words in our bodies and lives, we will always attract those things which correspond to our consciousness or sub-consciousness, in accordance with the *Law of Affinity*. This is made very clear by astrology, in which a certain astrological principle not only determines certain aspects of our character, but is also responsible for the kind of situations we "get into". What is remarkable is the fact that if we do not consciously live out a certain principle or suppress it and not integrate it into our lives, it will "happen" to us from the outside. Then when we are confronted by such a principle in some situation of life, we will be forced to come to terms with it. Every apparently coincidental situation reflects something of ourselves.

It is apparent that all things and events are part of a single unity and are as such interrelated, even though our senses only perceive the outerly visible expression of these things and their relationships to each other.

Therefore a holistic (*holos* is Greek for "whole") view of health, disease and healing is based on an assumption of the absolute unity of life in all its different forms of expression. And each symptom, whether physical, mental or psychological, is an exact indication of the point we have reached in our life's journey, making clear what remains to be learnt, what we have to come to terms with as well as pointing out those areas of ourselves we have pushed into one-sidedness and which we have to become reconciled to.

How is it possible that some people can apparently make the same mistakes as ourselves without having to suffer the same negative results. The further we travel on our path of development, the more clearly we recognize what we are lacking to become whole. Illnesses show us what steps have to be taken next in our personal evolution. They do not always need to be identical with those of other people. Each symptom is a specific message, which has to be recognized, accepted and integrated before we can get well again and take a step forward in our development at the same time. Illness always represents a chance and a need for growth.

For this reason, we are not meant to fight illness, but to recognise why it has occurred. By recognizing what we need to become whole, we are given the chance to consciously integrate what we are lacking and be led us back to a state of unity, "whole"-ness and holiness. When we manage to achieve this, the need for illness will become superfluous and we will be able to step away from polarity (and one-sidedness) to achieve a union of these two poles and as a result, health.

When people are asked what is the matter with them in Germany, they are literally asked "What are you *lacking*. What do you *lack?*" and the answer will generally not be what the patient is lacking but what he *has* such as a headache or a stiff back. This answer will generall indicate to a knowledgeable person what the patient *needs* in order to get well again.

Every disease has to dis-ease us, in order for us to change our ways. This means that illness provides fertile conditions for healing to take place and that every time we are healed, we are affirming holisitc development, which is the goal of all life. As Hermann Hesse says:

"By being accepted, misfortune can be turned into luck."
                                                                    Hermann Hesse
However, how can we understand the signals of a disease and integrate what

we are lacking into our consciousness when we are ill already. First of all, the most important thing will be to not reject the illness or suppress it, but to thank it for signalling to us that something is wrong.

If we aren't in a state of unity, this will be due to the fact that we continually suppress, reject, ignore or even fight certain areas of ourselves. However, when we reject or suppress something that exists within us, tension and pressure will arise and life will not be able to flow freely within us any more. What is more, pressure generates counterpressure. For example, if you are in a room and push against the walls because you want to get out into freedom, the more you press the walls, the more the counterpressure will increase and cost you energy. If you stopped pushing and took a look around you instead, you would discover that the room has a door. In this way you would be able to use your energy in a sensible and constructive manner instead of wasting it in a senseless fight.

Therefore, the first thing to do is to stop suppressing certain feelings and areas of ourselves and simply take a look at what is going on in us, without passing judgement. In this way, we can learn a lot about life.

If a stubborn child comes to you in need of help and feels that you condemn and reject it, it will never tell you what is the matter with it. Only when you pay such a child your whole attention and take on a loving approach will it be able to open up its soul. And often all that such a child needs is attention. Treat yourself, your life, your illnesses and your problems the same way as such a child. Pay loving attention to your pain, anger or fear without sitting in judgement over yourself and the fear these emotions hold over you and and the power they have over you will disappear. Be consequent and don't keep thinking "I can accept this but not that", "This is too painful and that is too terrible" and "It's all due to the virus anyway". Look at yourself and the way you react and accept yourself. When Jesus said:

> *"Resist not evil"*
> Matthew 5:39

and

> *"Love your enemies . . ."*
> Matthew 5:44

he was giving expression to a very great piece of wisdom. Only a person who does not resist can recognize the wholeness of life and the fact that it is a wonderful interplay of polarities. Indeed, creation is the result of the interaction of opposing powers alone and the person who has integrated this wholeness into himself is good by nature as well as being full of love and wisdom and joy and creative energy. It is suppression which brings about separation from the wholeness of life.

In the material world it is more sensible to expend one's energy on spreading light and love instead of fighting against the darkness, for where there is light, darkness will draw back of itself.

As you will have noticed in the course of this book, Reiki is a healing method eminently suited to bringing you back onto the path of wholeness. You will primarily experience a sense of relaxation with it, which will help you let go of tension, defensiveness and a sense of separation. However, this means that suppressed emotions and contents can often return to consciousness during treatment. In this case, welcome them and simply let them happen. With the help of the mental method you can also take influence on specific patterns of behaviour, as already described in Chapter 11. Since physical illness is always an expression of a psychological or spiritually false attitude in some sense, the symptoms involved will be able to tell us what is wrong with the ill person or what he is "lacking" as well as what he has suppressed or not integrated. With the help of the mental method we can treat his "lack" and help him become holistic, whole and healthy again.

Above and beyond this, each sick person can speed up his cure by taking a look at his inner self, as described beforehand, and fully accepting what he sees as well the way he reacts to discovering the cause of his illness. In this way he will be able to recognize and solve many problems.

In order to understand what is hidden behind a certain symptom in an intellectual sense, pay attention to the double meanings of some our expressions, for they will frequently point us in the right direction. In this way we will often be able to recognize the roots of a symptom while we are listening to someone. Unfortunately, this possibility has been reduced considerably by the introduction of latin designations for illnesses.

The interpretation of a symptom will be made easier if we ask ourselves in accordance to Dethlefsen *"What does this symptom force me to do and where does it impede me. In what circumstances did or does it occur"?* The answers to these questions will generally lead us to the basic problem and the central theme of the illness very quickly.

In addition, it is useful to know that if an illness is not paid attention to, it can slowly get worse in various stages. (Please compare to Dr. H.H. Reckeweg's Homo-toxine Theory and chapter 3). Illnesses usually begin with light functional disturbances and develop into acute physical ones such as bursitis, arthritis and otitis etc and all other inflammations (which end with *"itis")* as well as injuries and even little accidents. This stage is a very acute demand on the patient to understand and integrate something. If these symptoms are not paid attention to, chronic conditions like osteochondrolysis, gonarthrosis and arteriosclerosis etc. and all symptoms that end in *"sis"* will start to occur. The next stage will involve processes which are extremely difficult to heal, if at all, such as changes in the organs and cancer etc. If this phase of escalation is also not paid attention to, the final step will be death through illness or accident and congenital disturbance or deformation in a new cycle of development. This phenomenon is otherwise known as *karma*.

We have now come to the end of our brief excursion into the meaning of illness. It will no doubt be worth while to read this chapter several times in order to fully understand the contents and apply them to your life.

In order to help you when you start to apply this view of illness to actual cases, we have made up a list of symptoms and corresponding patterns of behaviour to help you or your patient back onto the path to health and wholeness. We do not lay claims to completeness and encourage you to make use of your own experience. The lectures of Thorwald Dethlefsen have provided us with much valuable insight into this topic and his explanations of illness coincide almost exactly with our own experiences with patients.

We are of the opinion that applying this list of interprations to the use of Reiki will be of unestimable value. If you have Second Degree Reiki you can complement the mental method with this knowledge and increase the effectivity of your work. Even without the Second Degree, the list will provide you with valuable insights and help clarify many a problem.

We recommend the following *literature* to those wishing to delve deeper into this theme.

"Bodymind" by Ken Dychtwald, Pantheon Books, 1977
"The Body Reveals — An Illustrated Guide to the Psychology of the Body", by Ron Kurtz and Hector Prestera, Harper Row Publishers, New York, 1979
"Your Face Never Lies An Introduction to Oriental Diagnosis" by Michio Kushi, Avery Publishing Group Inc., 1983

I have known both good and ill,
Sin and virtue,
Justice and injustice;
I have passed judgement
And been judged myself;
I have gone through
Death and birth,
Joy and sorrow,
Heaven and hell;
And in the end, I recognized
That I am part of everything
And that everything is part of me.

Hazrat Inayat Khan

Chapter 26

The Meaning of Symptoms from a Metaphysical Point of View

The following classification of symptoms according to the various parts of the body should not only assist you in looking them up but also help you understand that a single symptom is also part of a larger process. We have divided them in the following way:

1. Head
2. Throat
3. Respiratory System
4. Heart/Circulatory System
5. Digestion/Elimination
6. Generative System
7. Skin

8. Locomotive System
9. Infections
10. Allergies
11. Children's Diseases
12. Cancer
13. Psychological Problems
14. Miscellaneous

In reality, this kind of division into individual parts does not exist in reality, for all these parts are interrelated, and man should be regarded as a whole and not as a collection of individual organs, etc. In our opinion, even the division into somatic, physical, psychological and mental symptoms is not really justifiable, for all these symptoms are manifestations of one and the same problem or principle, differing only according to level. Therefore, it is important to always take the sum total of a person's symptoms into consideration.

UNITY

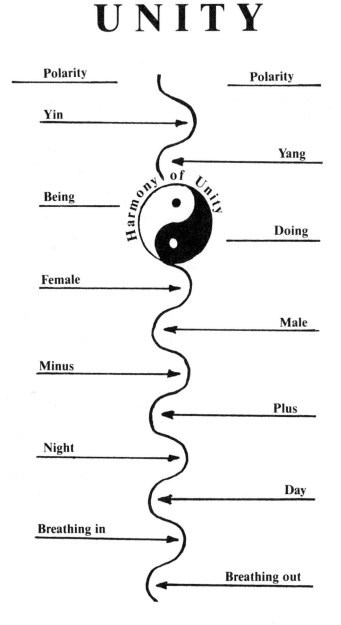

Only when both poles are balanced out will harmony and unity occur.

Head

Brain
Hair
Eyes
Nose
Ears
Mouth
Teeth and gums

BRAIN

Basic Factors
The right hemisphere of the brain predominantly controls the functions of the left half of the body and also has to do with faculties such as holistic understanding, creativity, feeling, intuition, sense of space and music. The right hemisphere also corresponds to the Yin of the Chinese as well as the moon, water, feminine aspects and the receptive.

The left hemisphere predominantly controls the right half of the body and has to do with the faculties of logic, analytical and rational thought, intelligence, language and mathematics. It also corresponds to the Chinese Yang, the sun, fire, masculine aspects and the principle of giving. (Please see the illustration on the previous page.)

Epilepsy
During an epileptic fit, a person lives out and releases suppressed energies and aggressions. The fit forces you to let yourself go, to allow yourself to fall and let go of both memories and consciousness. Accept the forces and energies inside you without condemning or suppressing them and give them a conscious look. Experience and accept whatever enters into your consciousness when you are falling asleep and just allow it to happen. This will help you learn the abilities of devotion and letting things go without having to be forced to.

Concussion

A concussion is something which shakes up your *whole means of thinking*. You are unable to hold your head upright because it begins to hurt as soon as you sit up. Let go of your old ways of thinking and go within yourself. Give yourself the chance of integrating feeling and intuition into your life.

Brain Tumour

A brain tumour is a means of making you realize that something must be changed about the way you think. You are too *hard-headed* and do not want to let go of old patterns of thought which have long since lost their validity. You should try to understand, however, that all life is subject to eternal change and that growth occurs where change takes place. Trust the flow of life — it will bring you to new shores more beautiful and rewarding than the present life you are leading. Trust the flow of life and you will find freedom.

Headaches

Headaches are an indication of excessive tension. They can be caused by the existence of strong external demands but also by excessive ambitiousness and striving for perfection. Other commom causes are *hard-headedness* or perpetual worrying (about things which literally *give you a headache)*. You are placing too much weight on rational thought and living in your head too much. Regain your balance by consciously following your inner feelings. Take your time and just allow things to develop of their own accord for a while. Accept what happens without judging it. This will release the tension and create space for peace, love and joy.

Migraine

Attacks of migraine indicate *resistance against the flow of life*. They arise out of the conflict between man's intellect and his natural urges, and show that a sexual problem has been forced to *come to a head*. Relax in the flow of life and accept and become aware of your sexuality and all the other energies you have within you. When they are no longer suppressed, you will discover that these energies are basically good and you will be able to make conscious and positive use of them and live them out to the fullest. If you are able to, give yourself increased Reiki in the head and genital area.

Apoplexy
During an attack of apopexly, the blood supply to a certain area of the brain is interrupted and the region affected ceases to function properly. This stands for extreme resistance to life and an inner negation of it at the same time. The resulting paralysis restricts your activity in the outer world. Accept this lesson and develop and pay more attention to your feelings and your intuition. Accept life in its entirety.

HAIR

Hair problems in general
Your hair is a symbol of freedom, strength and power. In earlier times, long hair was a sign of civic freedom, whereas short hair often signified that the power, freedom and dignity of the person in question had been *cut back*. (In this context, please see the Biblical story of Samson in Judges 16:17-31.) If you have problems with your hair, ask yourself what it is you really want to do, regardless of what other people expect of you. If you can find the courage to be true to yourself, you may regain your joy of living and thus also a sense of freedom and strength — as well as your hair. Developing this line of thought further may provide you with an interpretation for split or broken hair, too.

EYES

Eye problems in general
Our eyes are windows to the world and mirrors of our souls. They receive impressions and reflect in turn what we perceive. If you have problems with your eyes, you should ask yourself what it is that you do not want to see and you are closing your eyes to. Perfect clarity lies in the depths of your consciousness and it is here that you will be able to find both light and truth. Look within yourself, before turning your eyes to the world. In this way you will be able to form a different perspective of the things about you.

Conjunctivitis
Conjunctivitis indicates a conflict which you refuse to *look at consciously.*

If you feel the wish to close your eyes, then do so to look within. Be honest with yourself and face your conflicts. Look at them consciously and observe your reactions without condemning them. The solution lies within you already.

Blindness

Blindness is probably the most extreme form of not wanting to see. It is the manifestation of blindness of consciousness and forces the person affected to look within. Blindness can and should lead to inner *insight.* Look inside yourself of your own free will and find the things which are concealed from the eyes of the world. In this way you will discover a new world of your own and a new way of perceiving things.

Color Blindness

To a person who is color blind, everything seems *grey in grey* and looks the same. If you are unable to see the colorful diversity of life, open up your eyes to the unity which underlies it and take another look at the world again. You will soon realize how much joy and pleasure is to be found in the diversity of life.

Grey Cataract

When you have grey cataract, your vision is dimmed and things cannot be perceived clearly. In order not to see things that you don't want to, you maintain distance between yourself and your environment. It is as if you have *let down your blinds.* The reason why your outer vision has been dimmed is to help you stop regarding the external side of things alone. Therefore, if your future seems dark, look within until you find your inner light. This will then shed its light on the greyness of the outer world, just as the sun brightens up the greyness of a dull day.

Glaucoma

Glaucoma is the result of increased intra-ocular pressure. This in turn comes about as a result of continual inner pressure caused by the *tears that have not been shed* and the feelings that have been hurt. You have literally *lost sight* of the vastness and expansiveness of life. You only perceive a small section of the whole, and this corresponds to the patterns of thought you are caught up in. Admit to your grief and let the tears flow. After this, you will be able to open yourself up to the expanse and diversity of life again. As long as you cannot see what lies in the distance, turn to the depths within. Reiki is of great help in releasing pent-up emotions.

Short-Sightedness

Shortsightedness is always an indication of too much subjectivity. You regard everything from your *own point of view.* Your limited field of vision indicates that you should take a closer look at yourself, for doing so will lead you to increased self-knowledge. The world surrounding us is always an expression of ourselves. Therefore, what you see around you will teach you a lot about yourself and help you achieve more maturity. Your view of the world around you will also expand once you have discovered expanse within yourself. (For this reason, short-sightedness often disappears with the onset of old age. On the other hand, it can also develop at this time.)

Squinting

Squinting is a kind of one-sided vision, where you see everything from *one point of view* only and where things seem flat and two-dimensional. In order to become whole, you must try to get to know the other side of things and, above all, you must learn to accept. Try to take an unbiased view of reality without excluding certain aspects of it. Here again, disease will force us to be honest with ourselves, and show us what we are lacking at the same time. Pay attention to what your body is telling you and discover the beauty of being able to see all sides of life.

Far-Sightedness

Far-sightedness usually occurs in old age. It is an indication for us to see life as a whole and not remain caught up in trivialities. Follow the advice your eyes are giving you.

NOSE

Nasal Catarrh

Our nose is the organ with which we inhale and exhale the air we breathe.

A stuffed-up nose reduces this exchange with the environment. (Please see the **Respiratory System.**) When you have a cold, you want to retreat into yourself because you can't stand *the smell* of things anymore. Perhaps there are conflicts that you are trying to avoid or maybe things have simply become too much for you. Grant yourself the peace and rest you are yearning for, and allow yourself to place a distance between yourself and other people and problems. Gather new strength. You will then be able to clear up your conflicts with greater ease and awareness.

Sinus Problems

These symptoms indicate that someone close to you is irritating you. Observe the way you react and accept it. Give yourself a rest and regain your strength and independence. If you succeed in this, no one will be able to get on your nerves any more. Reiki can be a great help in this process.

EARS

Earache (otitis media or inflammation of the middle ear, for example)
As is the case with all inflammatory processes, this complaint is caused by a conflict which is not being lived out. In this specific instance, the conflict has to do with obedience. What is it you do not want to *hear?* In what area of your life do you lack humility? Complaints of this kind frequently occur in young children. Become aware of the fact that we unconsciously attract external situations and persons who teach us exactly the kinds of things we refuse to learn ourselves. Listen and learn, for everything has something to tell us. Listen to your inner voice, too, and follow its advice. This way you won't need to get earache.

Hardness of Hearing

This symptom usually occurs during advanced years. The person affected isolates himself more strongly than in the above case and becomes even more rigid and inflexible, for he is less willing to listen and obey. Although this complaint frequently occurs in the case of old people, this does not necessarily have to be the case. Like disease, old age brings out the truth, and problems which had not been solved earlier in life make a reappearance. Try to retain an *open and receptive* mind as you grow old and learn from everything that happens to you. Listen consciously to your inner voice, too, and just be open to all that comes.

Deafness
Only people who have closed themselves off to their inner voice for a long time become deaf. This is an extreme form of the symptoms described above, a state of extreme hard-headedness and isolation. By becoming deaf, you are absolutely forced to listen to what is going on inside you. Learn from this and listen to your inner signals and to the life flowing within you. Open yourself up completely to your inner voice and obey its commands.

MOUTH

Bad Breath
What you breathe out corresponds to the thoughts you carry around within you. If your breath smells unpleasant, this is because something you think is unpleasant, too. In this case, again, a complaint is facing you with the truth of the matter. Take a good look at the kind of thoughts you are mainly preoccupied with and realize that once love, friendliness and honesty prevail within you again, your breath will become fresh and your breath won't smell any more. Here again, Reiki will lead you to better knowledge of yourself.

General Mouth Complaints
Mouth complaints indicate a certain inability to *take in* new impressions and ideas. As a result, you are encumbered by rigid opinions and have become stuck. Learn to welcome unknown ideas and concepts and be prepared to accept the new. Become more flexible and open.

Adenoids
Adenoid problems are usually a sign of difficulties within the family and of a tense atmosphere in the home, while children who have this complaint generally feel rejected. Give your child the feeling that he or she is genuinely wanted, in spite of any difficulties which may exist. Every human being is an expression of the divine power of creation and has a right to be here, regardless of how much he or she may still have to learn. Accept yourself and your child as you are, and give each other real inwardly-felt love and affection.

TEETH AND GUMS

Teeth Problems in General, Including Tooth Decay

The condition of our teeth shows whether we are able to assert ourselves and *come to grips* with things and *bite our way through*. They also show whether we can *show our teeth*. Bad teeth are an indication that you have great difficulty in expressing your aggressions and the assertive side of yourself, and that you either do not want to recognize this fact or are unable to do so. You often have difficulty making decisions and suppress your natural aggressions for fear of losing love and recognition. Just be yourself, regardless of what people expect of you. Accept your aggressions and allow them to take place within you without condemning them. This way, they can be transformed into a positive, constructive force which will help you to attain your goals with ease. Be honest with yourself.

Grinding of the Teeth at Night

Grinding of the teeth at night is an indication of helpless aggressiveness. The desire to take *incisive* action is not admitted to during the day, therefore the excessive sharpness of the teeth has to be blunted away at night. It is time that you became aware of your anger, your aggression and your helplessness. Do not hide them away until you fall asleep. (For more information, please see **Tooth Problems**.)

Tartar (Odontolithiasis)

This complaint is a manifestation of aggressions which have not been dealt with and which have literally turned into stone. This means that if you solve your problems more consciously, it will not be necessary for them to manifest themselves through your teeth.

False Teeth

False teeth create an impression of vitality and assertiveness which in reality does not exist. If you have false teeth, take a look to see whether you have taken on *more than you can chew*, or whether you are living according to other people's expectations too much. Ask yourself what you really want, and have the courage to live it out.

General Complaints of the Gums

Just as the gums are the basis of the teeth, so are trust in life and self-confidence the basis of being able to assert oneself and *coming to grips* with things. Problems with the gums indicate an incapacity in this area, probably due to fear of losing love. You are touchy and vulnerable, and you don't have the courage to crack *hard nuts*. As soon as you love and accept yourself, you will no longer be dependent on the love and recognition of other people, and you will find the strength to realize your own wishes. You will become genuinely capable of giving to others the love you have found within yourself. Reiki will prove a great help in regaining your basic trust in life.

Throat

General Throat Problems
The throat is the passageway through which the air we breathe and the food we eat enter our bodies, as well as the means by which we verbally express ourselves. Throat complaints indicate not wanting or not being able to *swallow* something. They can also draw your attention to the fact that you have *swallowed down* anger, hurt feelings, etc. which you did not want to express. For this reason, throat complaints also have to do with fear to a certain extent.

Hoarseness (Laryngitis)
When you become hoarse, you are forced to withdraw from communication and confrontation. This can be caused by fear of being rejected when you *voice* your opinions. This symptom is a sign that you should learn to express your resentment and anger (often towards authorities) in a different way. The trouble you experience in the external world is only an expression of the conflicts within you. Take a rest, be alone for a while and look within yourself more. Once you are able to speak with love and trust again, you will no longer need to lose your voice. Treatment withReiki is very favorable in such cases and should be applied as often as possible.

Coughing (Please see under Respiratory System and Bronchitis)

Tonsilitis
When your tonsils are inflamed, it is difficult to swallow. There is something that you are no longer willing to accept and *swallow,* yet you suppress your feelings in spite of this, maybe because of fear of some kind. As in the case of all inflammatory processes, tonsilitis is an indication of an acute conflict which has been suppressed. You would be well advised to retreat and allow things to take their course for a while. Accept your feelings and your anger and take a look at your fear, too. With time, these feelings will cease to frighten you, and you will become open and free again.

Torticollis (Please see under **Locomotor System**)

Difficulties in Swallowing

If you have difficulty swallowing, or have a lump in your throat, you should ask yourself what it is you cannot or do not want to swallow. Accept your limitations. When something becomes too much for you, do not force yourself to go on just because others expect you to. Remember the peace and strength you have deep inside. Just be yourself and you will find it easier to "swallow."

Stiff Neck (Please see under **Locomotor System**)

Respiratory System

Breathing (in general)
Our breath links us not only to physical life but also to non-material realms. Breath integrates all forms of life and brings them into contact, for we all breathe the same air, whether friend or enemy, plant or animal. The respiratory system indicates the way we communicate and take up contact with the environment. At the same time, it also has to do with problems pertaining to freedom, as indicated by expressions such as **I can breathe freely again.** The act of breathing consists of inspiration and expiration, giving and taking. If you have difficulties with your breathing or with your lungs, ask yourself what it is you do not want to *take in* or *let out*. Maybe there is something you do not want to come into contact with. Perhaps you do not feel free in some respect or other. Reiki is a wonderful help in becoming more open to all aspects of life and taking part in a lively and open exchange, and, will also help you to accept and integrate life in its entirety.

Asthma
When you suffer from asthma, you take in a lot of air but you have difficulty letting it out again. Because you give out so little, it is soon impossible for you to take in enough and your breathing capacity gets smaller and smaller. You are probably someone who yearns for love but who has not yet learned how to give it. Always taking without giving does not work, however. What are you holding onto, what are you not willing to let go of? Do you have aggressions or anger that you have not admitted to yourself? Read Matthew 5:44 in the Bible and recognize that there is enough of everything for everyone. All that life has to offer is already present within you; it is only your present state of consciousness, your fear of not getting enough, which separates you from this knowledge. Give what you already have to others, and new life will start to flow in you again. Don't be afraid of admitting to your present state of helplessness and feelings of insignificance, for you will only receive help if you do. Become aware of what you have rejected and avoided so far. Accept and integrate life in its wholeness, and you will realize that there aren't any "enemies" any more — they were just a product of your conscious mind. You will finally be able to breathe freely again — a wonderful feeling.

Difficulty in Breathing

If your chest feels tight when you breathe in, or if you have difficulty getting air, ask yourself what it is that is *restricting* you and not allowing you to *breathe freely.* Find out, too, whether something has *taken your breath away or knocked you out of breath.* Accept the fact that you are a free person. Your real freedom lies within you, in your consciousness. It is up to you to let go of whatever it is that is oppressing you.

Bronchitis

Bronchitis indicates acute conflict and anger, or upset in the family or your immediate surroundings. The cough indicates that there is something that you unconsciously want to get rid of, something which is troubling you or making you angry. Realize that all the members of your family as well as everybody else are in the same school of life as you, and accept the fact that that each person has to follow his own path in life. Make peace with yourself and the life you are living. Live in joy.

Pneumonia

Pneumonia is a sign that the process of communication with life in all its aspects, including the non-material ones, is disturbed. You are caught up in a conflict with your ego and its attempts to hold its own and this conflict has made your lungs *flame up.* In many cases the person involved has been emotionally hurt and has retreated into himself as a result. Breathe in the breath of life again. It flows in sadness and joy alike, in the turbulence of life and in its states of balance and harmony. Reiki will be a very effective means of help in cases of pneumonia.

Tuberculosis

Tuberculosis of the lungs or consumption indicates a severe conflict between your egotism and and a living exchange with all life, a conflict which is *consuming* you. You want too much for yourself, and this has made you forget the wonderful breadth and variety of life. Breathe freely again and open yourself up to life in all its unity and difference, and realize that that there is enough of everything for everybody. To experience this, you just need to open yourself up to the wonder of every moment in life. Many sessions with Reiki will be helpful in this case.

The Heart and the Circulatory System

This section is divided into:
a) Heart
b) Blood
c) Circulatory System

Heart — Blood — Circulatory System (in general)
The heart is the physical symbol of our emotions and the capacity to love, while blood stands for vital energy and the joy of living. Our circulation distributes this vital energy and the joy of living throughout the body, with the help of the heart and its capacity for love and emotion. With Reiki, you will be able to open yourself up to the love within you and experience the joy and energy that lies both inside you and in all creation and be able to give it freely unto others.

HEART

Heart problems (in general)
In this case, as in so many others, expressions we use to describe things frequently indicates where the causes of heart symptoms lie, as when we talk of *heartlessness, hard-heartedness,* and doing things *half-heartedly* for example. These characteristics are usually the result of protracted emotional problems and a lack of joy, as well as rejection of life or in the belief that life is a fight for survival. Whoever recognizes these characteristics especially those with cardiac neurosis should *listen to the message of his heart more closely*. At the same time, ask yourself whether head and heart, intellect and emotions are in balance. Is there still a vital rhythm to your life? Do you live *with all your heart?* Are you able to *question your heart freely, or do you need to become ill first? If not, you won't need to have any heart problems.*

Heart Flutter
Heart flutter is an indication of emotional disturbance and a disruption in the order you have built up for yourself. Something is out of balance.

Whatever may have caused this disturbance, try to consciously integrate it into your life. *Take it to heart,* in other words.

Heart Attack

A heart attack indicates the release of a great accumulation of aggressive energy which has not been lived out. It is the sum total of everything which angers and annoys you and which, finding no other outlet, has now turned back on you with full force. Think of the fact that only a *hard heart* can break, and that it is the things that we cannot accept that *break our heart in two.* Take a conscious look at the pressure chamber of your non-lived-out emotions and do not sit over yourself in judgement. Open up your heart to yourself and others, and save yourself from having to have a heart attack.

Angina Pectoris

Constriction always has to do with fear and in the case of angina pectoris, expressions such as having a *hard heart, a cold heart* or a *heart of stone* are very telling. You have cut off your ego from the unity of life and your emotions are blocked as a result. Separation always causes antagonism or an attitude of defense. (Please see the Bible, Moses 15:7 and Hebrews 3:8.) This in turn creates fear, which you try to compensate for by striving for power. The physical expression of this mechanism is angina pectoris. When you close yourself off, nothing can enter or leave you, so open yourself up to the things you fear. Life is a process of continual exchange, and constriction and separation block you off from this. Give freely of the beauty within you.

BLOOD

Blood Problems (in general)

When you have problems with your blood, your body is showing you that joy is lacking in your life and that your ideas and thoughts cannot circulate freely. Why can't you see the beauty surrounding you? Why are you so blind to the positive side of life? Give your thoughts the freedom to partake of the beauty of life and allow them to flow freely.

Anæmia

Anæmia indicates a lack of joy and strength and a non- dynamic approach to life. Why do you refuse to make use of the energy that is yours by right? You should come to realize that there is enough strength, energy and joy for us all, and that we only need to open ourselves up to let it in. Reiki is the best example of this. It's time you changed your inner attitude from a "Yes, but" into a whole-hearted "YES."

CIRCULATORY SYSTEM

Arteriosclerosis

Arteriosclerosis indicates *resistance, tension, rigidity and narrow-mindedness.* Apparently you have become too inflexible, in both mind and body, and you are not aware of this. Now your body is trying to tell you quite clearly what your approach to life is lacking — namely *openness, flexibility, tolerance, affirmation of life and the world around us, as well as softness. Open yourself up* and go through life in peace, at one with yourself and the world.

Embolism

Embolism indicates that you are no longer innerly flexible and that you have become mentally rigid. Your life focuses too strongly on rest and relaxation and, as a result, your body has become lethargic. Realize that everything in life is in motion and that you are no exception to this. Be open and take on a flexible attitude, and become tolerant and loving in nature. Everything is in a state of flow. Join it.

High Blood Pressure

High blood pressure arises when you haven't expressed your thoughts and emotions over a long period of time. You are constantly living on the brink of conflict, without coming to any kind of conclusion. This naturally puts you under continual pressure. (This kind of problem is mentioned in the Bible, in Proverbs 13:12.) Take a good look at your problems and at whatever else is annoying you. Feel your way into them and live them out without holding onto anything. A conflict shows where you have to learn to let go.

This way you will be able to *let off* a great deal of pressure and face your problems again with a new kind of calmness. Reiki can help you in this process.

Low Blood Pressure
Low blood pressure is an indication that you try to avoid facing problems. You lack vital energy, stamina and cannot assert yourself. It can also indicate an attempt to avoid sexuality. Take a look at the forces at work within you, without passing any judgements. Simply observe what is going on and accept yourself with all your weaknesses. If you can be *honest* to yourself, you will find that you will also be able to face life and its responsibilities. Go within and discover that you are strong, too, then you will be able to enjoy being active. Reiki will provide you with additional energy if you have this complaint.

Varicose Veins
People suffering this condition often have an inner opposition to the work they do and don't like it at all. They feel overworked and even disappointed sometimes. The results are *lethargy, sluggishness and negativity* and may also involve lack of *elasticity, energy* and *inner support.* This is what your varicose veins are trying to tell you. It is important to accept your situation and the way you react to it. Be yourself again, then you will be able to *relax* and find a way of living your life in joy and inner fulfillment. Perhaps all you need to do is change your attitude and approach to the world. Once you have become free in this respect, your circulatory system will also be able to function freely again. Remember that your body is the expression of your thoughts.

Circulatory Collapse
Symptoms of this kind give you the opportunity to shirk responsibility and retreat from your problems instead of solving them. This way you can also use your helplessness to gain power over others. Once these symptoms subside, however, you will find that your problems are as overwhelming as ever. Admit to yourself that you have no power over certain situations and accept this fact. Then take a look at your problems without repressing anything. You will be able to find a solution this way and may even discover that you enjoy shouldering responsibility. (Compare please with **Fainting** and **Psychological Problems.**)

Oedema

Oedema indicates that you want to *hold onto* something. Maybe you are afraid of losing something but are not willing to admit to it. It is time that you let go of the past. Only the things that you hold onto, that you cannot or will not let go of, can be taken away from you. Whatever you give up of your own accord will return many times over.

Thrombosis

Thrombosis is a clear indication that your life does not *flow* enough and the result is stagnancy. There will usually be a certain amount of inner inflexibility, too. Your attitudes, opinions and ideas have solidified, and now your arteries are experiencing the physical manifestations of this problem. If this had not happened, you would never have realized that you were this way, but now you can become aware of it. Acknowledge and affirm the fact that nothing is static, and consciously let go of your *rigid opinions.* Grant yourself more inner and outer freedom, and your arteries will function properly again. Reiki is a wonderful way of encouraging the *flow of life* to start moving again.

Digestion and Elimination

a) Stomach
b) Intestines
c) Pancreas
d) Liver
e) Gall Bladder
f) Kidneys
g) Bladder

STOMACH

Stomach Complaints (in general)
The stomach takes in the food we eat and is the main organ of digestion. Therefore it stands for the *reception* and *digestion* of impressions. This in turn requires an attitude of *openness, acceptance* and *devotion.* If someone has banned the capacity for feeling from his conscious life, his stomach will have to live out his emotions instead. In order to open ourselves up to feelings and impressions, ideas and opinions and consciously integrate them, we need a sense of self-confidence and inner security. Stomach problems often point to problems in this area. Due to your lack of trust, you have difficulty accepting your feelings, particularly those of anger and aggression, and you find it difficult to face conflicts, too. Instead, you prefer to *swallow* things and let them *eat away at you.* Open yourself up to all that life has brought you and continues to bring. Once you come to realize that there is meaning behind everything that happens (and you will only be able to understand this meaning if you are open and receptive), nothing will *lie in your stomach like a stone* anymore and you won't find things so hard to *stomach* either. You will also learn to surrender yourself to life, with all its impressions and experiences, and you will be able to accept your feelings and freely express them, too.

Lack of Appetite
Lack of appetite is an indication that you are afraid of new *impressions* and that you refuse to accept the process of *digestion* that goes along with them. This is most evident when something *spoils* your *appetite.* The world is full

of new and exciting impressions, and if you turn your back on them you will only be half alive. Try to increase your inner capacity for receiving impressions and your appetite will improve of itself.

Gastric Ulcers

Gastric ulcers occur when a person cannot vent his feelings and aggressions and turns them on himself instead. This is a kind of self-destruction, for the stomach starts to be digested by its own gastric juices. Accept your feelings and stop avoiding conflicts. Open yourself up to impressions from the outside and consciously *digest* them and accept your aggressions, too. Admit to your yearning for motherly protection and warmth as well as your desire to be loved and cared for. (See also under **Heartburn.**)

Heartburn

If you *swallow* your anger again and again, your gastric juices will become very *acid* in an unconscious attempt to give vent to your feelings, and the result is heartburn. At the same time, however, heartburn also creates a feeling of presssure which prevents the intake of further food. You are obviously *sick* and tired of *swallowing* whatever it is that annoys you. Realize that there is a meaning to everything in life, including the way you react. Understanding this will give you a feeling of trust and security which will help you express your needs and anger (if it is still there) more freely in future.

Nausea (and vomiting)

Nausea always indicates rejection of something we find too hard to *digest,* not only in the physical sense. If we eat too many different foods or take in too many different ideas, we will not be able to *digest* them sufficiently, and vomiting will prevent us from taking in any more. Nausea and vomiting during pregnancy, however, generally means unwillingness to *receive* the semen which produced the child but can also mean rejection of one's own femininity, or even of the child itself. Whatever the case, be a little more conscious of what you *take in* and make sure that it is *digestable.* When you become nauseous your body is merely trying to show you that taking in too much of something is not a good idea. If you are unable to change the situation you are in, increase your capacity for breadth and openness within, and you will be able to *receive* more. Thank your body for what it is telling you.

INTESTINAL TRACT

Flatulency
These symptoms are often due to the fact that you cannot or do not want to *swallow* something. At the same time, there is an unwillingness to admit to this and, therefore, by swallowing air, you simulate the act of real swallowing. Another cause could be that you have taken in too many things that do not agree with you and they are now bloating you up. You should become more discriminating and only take in what you want and what you can digest properly. Accept yourself as you are, including any limitations you may have, and learn to say "no." You will be able to relax inwardly again and life will be able to flow *through* you easier.

Appendicitis
Like all inflammatory processes, appendicitis indicates that there is an urgent, acute problem which is blocking the flow of life, frequently coupled with a fear of life itself. Stop stemming yourself against the things that happen to you. Observe and accept them and let life takes its course. Reiki will be a big help to you in this process.

Intestinal Spasms
Cramps and colics frequently indicate tension which has come about through a person's holding onto outlived phases of development, a state which results in intestinal congestion and stomach cramps. You must learn to let go of those things which are no longer valid for your development. The tension will then slacken by itself or not even need to arise. Just let go, be open for the new and allow your life to *flow.*

Catarrhal Colitis (Colitis ulcerosa)
You probably had very exacting and strict parents and experienced a lot of repression and humiliation with the result that you are afraid of unfolding your own personality and often play a role just to please others. As you have an excessively strong need for affection, you attach yourself too strongly to others instead of living out your own life. Have the courage to be yourself. If you can accept and love yourself, you will free yourself of your dependency on others and come to realize that life is an enjoyable process.

Diarrhea (acute and chronic cases)
Fear is usually involved in cases of diarrhea, as several colloquial expressions such as *he shat in his pants* prove. In some cases it may be that you simply want to get rid of something instead of accepting and digesting it, maybe something from the past. Perhaps you simply let new impressions *pass through* you without *digesting* them because they are too overwhelming, as is often the case when we travel through foreign countries. All experiences and impressions have something beautiful and useful to give you. Open yourself to them without fear and take them in.

Haemorrhoids
This symptom shows that you have problems letting go, that something is oppressing you which you cannot or will not let go of. Try to take a conscious look at whatever it is that frightens you and do this without fear. Do not side-step your problem, but go through it again without condemning anything. As soon as you can fully accept the problem you have, you will feel light and unburdened and able to live in the here and now again without the need for hæmorrhoids.

Digestive Complaints (in general/small intestine)

The small intestine analyzes and evaluates the food we eat and is therefore a symbol of the analysis and *digestion* of impressions and of criticism. Fundamental fear is also typical of complaints of this kind, especially the fear of not being able to get enough. You probably lack a sense of security and have a lot to criticize. If you can succeed in adopting a more open attitude you will be able to deal with all new impressions more easily, without having to suffer physically. Learn not to take minor issues so seriously and devote yourself to the *game of life* with more enthusiasm.

Constipation (large intestine)

Constipation is a striking manifestation of a psychological problem on the physical level. It often has to do with greediness and stinginess and your wanting to *hold onto* things, usually material things. You probably have difficulty in letting go of old ideas, too, as well as an accompanying fear of letting repressed problems come to the surface. You are constipated, both mentally and physically, and cannot leave certain things *behind* you, as your complaint proves. It is evident that you must learn to let go. Let go of the past and of your stinginess, leave outlived ideals behind you and stop repressing things which you find uncomfortable to deal with. Allow life to *flow through* you generously again and you will find the security and riches you are seeking within.

Duodenal Ulcer
Directing your aggressions against yourself again and again will give rise to tension, fear, anxiety and pressure which will begin to *eat you up*. What is the best way of dealing with aggression. Either you live it out, which should only be done if others are not hurt in the process — or you simply observe *that* you are aggressive and let it be without condemning yourself or passing judgements. After a while your aggression will *burn* itself *out* and your physical complaint will begin to disappear. In this case, Reiki is an excellent means of neutralizing tension and will help you to become peaceful and harmonious again.

PANCREAS

Diabetes
At the root of this disease is frequently a wish for love, paired at the same time with the inability to let oneself be loved. Hyperacidity is the result, for *those who do not love turn sour* while *those who cannot enjoy are no joy to have around.* You are lacking in the *sweetness of life* and yearn for the love you are unable to give. Let go of the past and accept that fun and games and love and affection are fundamental basics of life.

LIVER

Liver Complaints (in general)
The main tasks of the liver are metabolism (of carbohydrates and proteins) and detoxication. It also analyzes and evaluates what is of benefit to the body and what is not. Thus, on a psychological and spiritual level, the liver

has to do with analysis, evaluation and judgement, as well as measure, proportion and excess. The liver converts animal and vegetable protein into human protein, whereby the basic substances remain the same. Thus, this organ creates a higher form out of a lower, and is, therefore, a symbol of the realm of higher development and evolution. During this process, the amino acids, which are basic substances, remain unaltered, although their structure or form of manifestation is changed. In the same way, the manifold forms of life are merely different manifestations of one underlying being. The liver is an expression of this fact and is, therefore, also associated with *religio,* or *reconnection with the source of being* (in accordance with Dethlefsen). If you have problems with the liver, you ought to ask yourself whether you are doing something excessively in an area of your life, and whether this is perhaps not good for you, if not even *poisonous.* Are your standards of judgement still *measured* and appropriate, or are you annoyed about a lot of things and complain about them? Are you *liverish?* Are your ideals too high? And what about your relationship to your innermost self? In answering these questions, you will soon discover where your liver problem lies. Truth is simplicity, so let go of everything that is *too much* for you and find the freedom, understanding, love and trust that is within you. Reiki will help you to discover and make use of these qualities.

Jaundice
You exaggerate things, are very biased and have strongly *colored opinions.* Become more tolerant and *balanced out* and give your love and sympathy to all persons. Your jaundice is trying to tell you to let go of your one-sided attitude. If you are able to, give yourself Reiki. (Please also see under **Liver Problems** in general.)

Hepatitis
Heptatis is an indication of acute conflict. Ask yourself whether you are lacking in objective judgement and whether anger, fear and resentment have risen in you as a result. Have you become one-sided or gone too far in some way? Whatever the case, your hepatitis is now enforcing you to rest and restriction.
Use this time well and let go of everything, including criticism, anger and old ideas. This is the chance to make a new start. (Please see under **Liver Problems.)**

Cirrhosis of the Liver

If you read the interpretations of the liver complaints described above, you will be able to recognize where the causes of this condition lie. In this case, however, the problems involved have escalated to a further stage. Apparently you were never willing to learn from earlier symptoms and did not draw the necessary consequences. Nothing has changed as far as your inner life and your opinions are concerned. Your body is now calling on you, for perhaps the last time, to change your course. Your consciousness is the ruler of your body. Make up your mind soon.

GALL BLADDER

Gall Bladder Complaints (in general)

Bile is an extremely aggressive substance which breaks up fats. Gall bladder complaints always have to do with aggression and it is obvious that you are not fully aware of the fact that you are aggressive, regardless of whether you live this out or not. Symptoms of this kind usually indicate pent-up aggression and blocked energy. The typical choleric is *bilious* by nature because he does not live out his energies consciously. Take a conscious look at whatever raises your anger without passing judgement on yourself. Be honest, and accept both yourself and your power. Your anger will dissolve, and you will be able to make positive use of all this energy.

Gallstones

Here the symptoms described above have reached a further state of development. *Bitterness, hard* feelings and aggressions have now turned to *stone*. It is probable that your life stands under the influence of compulsive forces. Open yourself to life in all its *sweetness* and let go of the past. It is up to you to decide whether you want to live the rest of your life in bitterness or whether you will allow true love to develop within you. Reiki will certainly be of help in coming to the right decision.

KIDNEYS

Kidney Complaints (in general)

Like all organs arranged in pairs, the kidneys have to do with the idea of partnership. While the lungs represent the realm of friendship and communication, and the testes and ovaries stand for sexual relationships and eros, the kidneys have to do with complementation, with living out an unconscious part of ourselves through a partner. Usually we attract people who represent our *shadow,* that aspect of ourselves which we would like to be (or repress) but which we have not yet integrated. If you have problems with your kidneys, it is probable that you project your deficiencies and problems onto your partner or other people. As a result you are very sensitive, often disappointed and frustrated and critical of others. In the same way that your body will become poisoned if the kidneys do not properly discriminate waste products, you will poison yourself if you project your problems onto others instead of solving them yourself. You should ask yourself what your problems with partnership are and what limitations they are trying to show you. Accept whatever you happen to find, for only in this way will you be able to learn. Everything we encounter outside ourselves which calls forth a reaction within us enables us to gain self-knowledge, growth and maturity. In this way, life itself becomes a partner. Open yourself to this potential and stop clinging to old problems. Reiki will help you to experience the love and joy within yourself and then you will be able to find it in the world about you.

Pyelonephritis

As is the case with all inflammatory diseases, this complaint indicates an acute problem or an urgent conflict in the realm of partnership or relationship which you have not yet consciously solved. Now the conflict has *taken hold* of your kidneys and is calling for your attention. Take a look at your problem and at everything that has to do with it. Try to accept and deal with these matters in a conscious way. (Please also see the information under **Kidney Problems.**)

Kidney Stones

Kidney stones are the result of aggressions in your partnership which have been held onto so long that they have solidified. It is probable that you cling tenaciously to problems and negative thoughts which are old and outlived, instead of letting them go. In doing so, you have brought your development to a halt. Ask yourself what old problems you are clinging to, for they are impeding the natural flow of your development. Make use of the chance now being offered you to leave the past behind. Give your kidneys love in the form of Reiki.

Atrophic Kidneys (also applicable to dialysis patients and people with artificial kidneys.)
If the problems which have been described above are not dealt with and consciously integrated, it is likely that you will arrive at this last stage. Your new partner is now a dialyser, however, a machine for washing out your blood. An intimate partnership, indeed, for now you are truly dependent. At the same time, however, you have the chance of realizing that you will never find the perfect partner until you have become perfect yourself. It is very important for you to develop love and affection within yourself and not to project your problems onto others. (Please see the remarks under **Kidney problems** in general.)

BLADDER

Cystitis
The substances secreted by the kidneys are conducted to the bladder, where they wait to be discharged or released until enough pressure has built up. In the case of cystitis, the process of releasing and letting go is linked with pain. *In spite of great pressure, you can hardly let go of anything.* This inability is being demonstrated in a very clear and acute manner, for cystitis is an inflammatory process. Perhaps you have been putting yourself *under pressure* lately and are now projecting it onto others. It would be better to voluntarily *release* old psychological contents and *let them go,* for they are merely dead weight. Go through all the attitudes and opinions you have become used to and discover what you have been *holding on to* out of fear. If you do this and discard unnecessary opinions, etc., you will not need to have cystitis any more.

Weakness of the Bladder (in general)
Anticipatory anxiety of long standing gives rise to weakness of the bladder.

You apparently *push* psychological pressure *down* to the bladder where it soon makes itself felt. You should realize that *letting go of pressure* always brings relief. Learn to *relieve yourself* of psychological pressure and your bladder will take care of itself.

Nervous or Irrritable Bladder

A nervous or irritable bladder indicates *long-standing pressure* which has been *pushed down* to the bladder because it has not been consciously dealt with. Take a look at your most *pressing* problems and face them squarely. You will then be able to transform the pressure that is *irritating* you and become free and content again.

Generative System

a) Pregnancy and Birth
b) Sexual Problems
c) Other Complaints

PREGNANCY AND BIRTH

Miscarriages (in general)

When a miscarriage occurs, it is probable that the child is being consciously or unconsciously rejected. Often there will be underlying domestic conflicts or tension. Here again, "disease" shows us where the truth lies. If you really want a child, make it truly welcome and its birth will become an overwhelmingly positive experience for both mother and child.

Premature Birth

A premature birth may indicate that the mother wanted to get rid of the child before the time of birth but could not or did not want to admit this to herself. Naturally, this is a fact which is generally denied. Frequently there will be an unconscious aversion against a further pregnancy, too. The premature birth reveals what you were trying to hide. If you want to avoid having a premature baby, give your unborn child all your love and attention as well as a lot of Reiki.

Pseudo or Phantom Pregnancy

Pseudo pregnancy indicates a strong wish for a child, on the one hand, and unconscious fear of the responsibility, on the other. In the case of women who live alone, a pseudo pregnancy usually represents the wish to have someone to love without having to *bear* the aspect of sex which goes with a relationship. Responsibility and sex are areas of life which can become both beautiful and fulfilling if you open yourself up to them and live with them consciously. If you can completely affirm these areas of life, your external circumstances will change accordingly, for like attracts like.

Complaints during Pregnancy (in general)

When a woman has complaints during pregnancy, it is often because she rejects the child within her, to a certain extent. The more she denies it, the more it is likely to hold true. We are not trying to pass judgement or say that this is good and that is bad, rather, we are concerned with honesty and every symptom you display has to do with the truth. Try to find out why you reject your child. It is quite apparent that you both have something to learn from each other. Open yourself up to what is about to happen to you and accept the situation as it is. This will enable you to love your unborn child more. It is a wonderful thing to experience new life growing within you. (Please see chapter 9, "Using Reiki with Babies.")

Delayed Birth

A delayed or post-term birth is the opposite of a premature one, for here the mother refuses to let the child go. The same problem may arise again when the child becomes adult and tries to leave home. We must learn to let go of what we cling to, even if it is an unborn child. The more you give, the more you receive. If you can live this out, it will bring you a great sense of freedom and blessing. *"It is more blessed to give than to receive."* (The Acts of the Apostles, 20:35)

SEXUAL PROBLEMS

Frigidity

If you are frigid, you cannot or will not give yourself to your partner, or you do not want to take a *subordinate* position. It may also be that you are afraid of your sexual urges and wishes or do not want to appear indecent, and this prevents you from *giving and receiving*. You prefer to remain *cool* and frigid instead. Devotion always entails opening oneself up and letting things in, and there are many things that can only be experienced in their full depth and beauty in this way. This also holds true for sexuality. Learn to accept your sexual feelings and don't allow your fear or rejection of them to make them into something ugly.

Venereal Disease

Practically all venereal diseases prevent sexual intercourse in one way or another, therefore they also suggest the idea of self-punishment. There is usually a sense of guilt concerning sex combined with the belief that the genitals are *dirty and* even *sinful.* Take a break, and realize that sexuality will become pure and beautiful if you can accept it as being an expression of love and a wish for union. If you can do this, you will have no feelings of guilt or fear of punishment.

Impotency
Problems pertaining to potency always have to do with fear of letting go and losing control, as well as fear of repressed psychological contents. The necessary energy is kept in the head instead of going to where it is needed. There will often be feelings of sexual pressure and tension, as well as ones of guilt, and some even feel, spite against an earlier partner. It isn't surprising that everything goes wrong. Once you have become more conscious of these things you will realize that it is necessary to go into your feelings more, for sex has nothing to do with the intellect. Either give of your innermost or give nothing at all. If you can let go of your mind, you will soon experience the power of emotion and the joy of sexual energy.

Vaginal Spasms (Vaginismus)
You are either trying to *hold onto* the person you love or you are afraid of losing him (or someone else). Feelings of guilt concerning sexuality could also play a role. Realize that you only need to let go and that nothing ever gets lost, not even true love. Realize, too, that all parts of you are beautiful.

Sexual Perversion (Please see under PSYCHE)

VARIOUS OTHER COMPLAINTS

Female Breast (Soreness and Cysts)
These symptoms call to your attention that your motherly instincts have become somewhat too strong and that you have become domineering and arrogant. Since you are not aware of this, your body is calling your attention to it. Accept that we are all free individuals and that each of us must find and pursue his own path in life. Allow yourself and others to be free and independent.

Menstrual Complaints (in general)
Menstrual complaints are an inner protest against true devotion and an unconscious resistance against femininity, sex and the male partner. There are often feelings of guilt, and sexuality is regarded as being something sinful and unclean. To be a woman means to experience and develop the power of devotion receptivity and love. These characteristics form an important contrast to the male powers of resistance and assertion (yang forces) which are so predominant in the world today. Become aware of the beauty and strength that lie in being a woman and accept your femininity. Reiki will help you to *open yourself up* to being a woman.

Complaints of the Prostrate Gland
Complaints of this nature are an indication that your consciousness has become colored by various false judgements and opinions. Belief in failure and fear of becoming older and having to renounce important goals in life also form the background to this kind of symptom. With your pessimistic attitude you often tend to place the blame on others while sexual tension and unconscious feelings of guilt also play a role. Reiki can be a great help in regaining access to the inexhaustable source of strength that lies inside you. If you learn to accept your creative male energy in all areas of your life, you will be able to enjoy sex again.

Sterility
Sterility in some women indicates an unconscious rejection of pregnancy, while in others a child is only wanted as a means of binding the partner, indicating an underlying trait of dishonesty. Male sterility indicates fear of close relationship as well of having to bear responsibility for the child. In both cases, it is important to be honest with yourself and admit to what you really want, without condemning your wishes. You will then be able to take the right step forward.

Inflammatory Complaints
As is the case with all inflammatory complaints, the body is here urging you to solve consciously a sexual problem which has long been repressed. This problem could concern feelings of guilt, of having lost a beloved person or of something you value very highly. Become aware of your inner conflict and take an honest look at it. You will discover that it is not so hard to let go. True love is something which can never be lost, so there is no need to

cling to it. And love has nothing to do with guilt, not even in the sexual aspect.

Climacteric Complaints (Menopause)

An entire complex of symptoms are contained within menopause problems. In the background, there will often be problems such as the fear of growing old, the fear of no longer being attractive and desirable, as well as a certain self-rejection. Some women get *hot flashes* which prove that they are still pretty *hot,* while the reappearance of menstruation represents the longing for youthfulness and fertility again. Remember that only things that have not been lived out can get you *all hot and bothered,* while things you have gone through will leave you *cold.* Live according to your natural needs, regardless of social expectations and artificial concepts of morality. Observe the changes you are going through and recognize that they are neither good nor bad. Change is life and life is growth. Enter into this new cycle of development with a feeling of openness and joy.

Skin

Skin Problems (in general)
The skin is the organ which encloses our bodies, the boundary between inside and outside. It is our skin which comes into direct contact with the world and for this reason it is a symbol for making contact and drawing the line between ourselves and others. The way your skin looks and the state it is in says a lot about you as a person. Over-sensitive people often have *sensitive* skin, while the opposite is true of the *thick-skinned*. Skin that is moist from perspiration indicates insecurity or fear while a person who is always flushed is probably excitable. The "boundary" of the skin can broken through from within by means of a **rash** or **abcess** or from without by means of an **injury.**
If you have problems with your skin, you should always ask yourself the following questions? Are you able to make contact with others? Are you able to give or receive tenderness? Do you set too definite limits and, if so, is something trying to *break* or *bore* its way through these limits?
The full Reiki treatment will help you to break through the boundaries you have set up between yourself and the world so that you can enter into a loving relationship with the people around you. You can support this by means of the mental method and by treating the affected areas directly.

Abscess
Since an inner conflict has not been able to find release on the psychological level, it is now doing so on the physical one, and the result is that your skin *erupts* and is *inflamed.* You are now physically experiencing the pain and danger of the conflict you have been avoiding. It would be better for you if you lived out your conflicts consciously instead of trying to avoid them. If you attempt to solve things of your own free will, they will not have to manifest themselves in such an uncomfortable way.

Acne
If you suffer from acne, it is a sign that something inside you, which you have been suppressing out of fear, insecurity or shame, is trying to *break through* and *become visible.* If you are a teenager, it is probable that you are suppressing your sexuality out of fear of the unknown, for acne is a sign of unconscious resistance to *close* contact with others, even if this is what you

are yearning for. This manifestation of your inner conflict is a hint to overcome the boundaries set by your *ego* and to find someone you can be close to. Accept all the forces and changes going on inside you, and recognize that sexuality is beautiful and natural. Open yourself up, and you will find that very special person.

Eczema

Eczema is an indication that an emotional or unconscious factor is *irritating* you and must be dealt with consciously. You may also be resisting something; maybe you feel threatened or hurt. These feelings can only come about, however, when you erect barriers and try to draw the line too strongly between yourself and others. Become aware of what is causing this irritation and integrate it into your life. Once you no longer need to erect such barriers, you will be able to love and understand what you once found so threatening.

Furuncles (Boils)

A furuncle is an indication of an acute problem which is making you very angry, literally bringing you *to the boil*. If you know how to give yourself Reiki, sit down and lay your hands on your solar plexus for a while and give your anger free rein. Don't suppress it, but just observe it until it doesn't interest you any more. Take a good look, for this is an interesting phenomenon. All of a sudden, your feelings of anger will vanish and your furuncle will become superfluous.

Ulcers

You are oppressed by something and gnawed away at by fear and tension. Take a square look at whatever is causing these feelings. Observe how you react, without evading anything. You will soon realize that the fear and tension have disappeared and that you are becoming peaceful and optimistic again. Your ulcer will soon disappear, too.

Shingles (Herpes zoster)

Shingles point to long-standing tension, uncertainty and indecision. The associated pain stems from aggressions which have not been given vent to and which have now turned on you in self-aggression instead. (Please see Galations, 6:7.) Try to find out where your uncertainty comes from and ask yourself where you are unable to make decisions. Trust the flow of life; accept what happens. You will soon find guidance. Have trust that things will develop in the best possible way.

Rashes

A rash may be an indication that you feel threatened within the boundaries you have set yourself and that you are now *striking back* in order to protect yourself. At the same time, you are trying to attract attention. Your insecurity has caused you to *suppress* your emotions and now they are forcibly making themselves felt. However, you will only feel threatened if you close yourself off. Reiki can help you win back your confidence and become aware of your suppressed feelings. Be open towards yourself and you will be able to open yourself up to others and receive attention which is gladly given.

Itching

Something is *itching* you and really *getting on your nerves.* Perhaps this is an unfulfilled wish, an unconscious yearning for physical closeness, or else feelings of anger. Something is urging its way outwards and demands to be acknowledged. It would be better to *scratch around* inside yourself for a while to find what is *itching* you. Realize that your wishes and anger are expressions of your basic liveliness and don't project them onto others.

Milk crust (eczema in babies)

If your baby has milk crust, it is trying to show you that it needs more emotional warmth and physical contact. This is the child's attempt to *break through* its feeling of isolation. Give your child more attention and love. Take him in your arms and stroke him, and give him as much Reiki as possible.

Psoriasis

Psoriasis is like a suit of armor which is laid on by particularly sensitive people out of fear of emotional injury. *Nothing can be let in or out with this impenetrable armour.* These symptoms manifest a yearning for closeness and, at the same time, a fear of intimacy. The cracks and sores are an indication that you have to *open* yourself up, even if this means becoming vulnerable. Open yourself up to life in whatever form you encounter it. Be prepared for the injuries and pain that can happen to you, but don't get frightened and close yourself off. Simply observe that they can happen and they will soon stop causing you pain. Show your feelings freely again and be receptive to others.

Burns (external)

A burn is an injury to the skin, which is the boundary between an individual and the world about him. In order to be able to really love, these boundaries have to be pushed aside. Perhaps you have burnt yourself because you have a *burning desire* for love, which you are not prepared to grant yourself. Perhaps you have used the *fire of life* wrongly, and now you are *flaming* mad. Another possibility could be that you have misjudged dangers and *burnt your fingers* as a result. Fire is the living expression of energy, and, when this energy takes on the form of love, it will *melt your heart.* Allow this to happen to yourself. On the other hand, if you are *burning* with anger, sit down and just take a look at what is going on, without projecting your feelings onto others. After your anger has *flamed up* a while, it will will gradually *go up in smoke* and make space again for peace, harmony and the *glow* of love.

Warts

Warts are an indication that you find an inner aspect of yourself ugly and that this makes you feel guilty. Realize that everything inside you is an expression of the *game of life* in all its variations. For this reason, everything has a right to be and is beautiful in its own way, especially if you cease to condemn what you don't like. You, too, are beautiful and worthy of love. Once you have realized this, you won't need to have warts any more.

Locomotor System (in general)

The locomotor system of the body (i.e., the moving parts) symbolizes mobility and flexibility as well as *bearing* and *poise*, both inner and outer. For example, we speak of some people as being *upright* and of others as being *stiff-necked*, while we find that old people are often *bowed* with age. The locomotor system itself consists of bones, muscles, sinews and ligaments. The bones form the inner framework and lend the body *support*, and for this reason, they represent stability and the moral standards which give us support as human beings. When these standards become too rigid for example, our bones get easily broken or they become brittle. Our muscles and extremities symbolize mobility and activity. With the help of our hands we can grasp or hold things and, therefore, our hands stand for the ability to *grasp* or comprehend things and to *take a hold* on them. With our legs on the other hand, we make our *progress* through life and problems in this area point to inner difficulties in this sense. *Bending* our knees has to do with humility and therefore the knees have to do with this too. We use our feet to stand on the ground, some of us more firmly and some of us less. Therefore feet have to do with *stability* and *being able to stand one's ground* as well as with humility and understanding.

Acidosis
Acidosis indicates that *undigested* matter, which you have not been willing to solve or resolve, has accumulated in your unconscious and is now making your body so hyperacid that even genuine physical compaints like **rheumatism** can develop. However, repressing things like this is no solution, even if it appears to be so. Take a look at your problems, and at whatever else is irritating you instead, and try to deal with them consciously, without repressing anything. If you succeed in *solving* something on a conscious level, you won't need to suffer it on a physical one. While treating acidosis can be quite painful, *solving* problems and resolving conflicts will bring you both joy and a sense of liberation.

Stiffness of Old Age (in general)
Stiffness of old age generally occurs when the individual involved is unaware of being *rigid* or of having too narrow standards. Instead, he *rigidly* adheres to certain principles and is mentally *inflexible* and unable to accept change.

Let go of your rigid concepts and principles, and your body will become free and flexible again. Become open!

Arthritis (in general)

Arthritis forces you to rest and compensate for over-activity on a physical level, for inwardly you have become *rigid, hard-headed* and *stubborn.* Try to face up to this fact with honesty. Perhaps you are also overly moralistic and fastidious. Bitterness, resentment and ill humor will be the results, and you will feel basically unloved. Yet love is everywhere, you simply need to open yourself up and let it in. Be friendly, loving and understanding with yourself, and then you will be this way with others, and they will treat you the same way in return (in accordance with the Law of Affinity). Be free and grant others the same right to freedom. Genuinely forgive is also to love.

Arthrosis (in general)
Arthrosis is an escalation of the symptoms mentioned under **Arthritis.** The person suffering from arthrosis adheres even more *rigidly* to his concepts and opinions, however, with the result that he finally *seizes up* and begins to *rust.* Inner flexibility will gradually restore physical *mobility.* The whole of creation is continually *in movement,* taking part in the joyous dance of life. Join in. Get moving.

Slipped Disks (Disc Protrusion)
This condition shows a certain indecision which is often associated with the feeling of not getting enough emotional *support.* Something has *blocked up* inside you, and you have become *stiff* and *immobile.* Perhaps you have *taken on too much* in your search for love and recognition, and now find yourself under considerable *pressure.* With a slipped disk, you are forced to rest and this is a good opportunity to take a look at your situation and arrange things anew. Have the courage to be independent of the opinions of others, and open yourself up to life, both inner and outer. You will soon become flexible and free again. If you trust in life, it will *support* you too, so be open for this support.

Leg Problems (in general)
With the help of our legs we *stride towards the future,* and if you are afraid
of the future, or believe that your life cannot go on this way, without admitting it to yourself your legs will start to make themselves felt and hold you
up in your *further progress.* Look at your situation consciously and admit
to your fear or, whatever feelings of resistance you may have. If it is not
possible to make any external progress, go within, find peace and strength,
and ask yourself what you really want and what can be achieved without too
much difficulty. Stick to your decision and *undertake* any *necessary steps.*
This way you will be able to *walk through life* with optimism and joy again.
(See also under **Foot Problems.**)

Weakness of the Connective Tissue (in general)
Weakness of the connective tissue always indicates a certain lack of inner
posture and mental vigor. This is why you are so easily *hurt* and slow to
forget any slight you have received, as evidenced by the bruises which you
get after every little *bump.* Ask yourself what you really want and remain
true to yourself and your innermost wishes, then you will find more inner
support and *strength.* Don't always be the one to *give in.* Be yourself; you will
no longer be dependent on the love of other people. You will discover the
wealth of love and beauty that lies within the depths of your being and will
be able to pass this onto others.

Brittle Bones
Our bones support us, just as moral standards do. When the latter become
too *rigid* and limited, our bones will react accordingly. Let go of your inner
rigidity and the narrow standards which govern your life. Let go of them
consciously and let things happen; allow yourself to drift and learn to accept
without passing judgement. This way you will become *flexible* and *adap-
table* again.

Curvature of the Spine (Hunchback)
A pronounced curvature of the back indicates that you should live a life of
humility. Since this quality is lacking in you, anger and irritation have
accumulated in your back and are clearly showing you what you lack in your
conscious attitude. If you were born with a strong curvature of the spine, it
is your task to learn humility and integrate it into your life. You have made

this choice yourself and you should accept it. Everything is well and good as it is, and you should realize that no one has ever harmed you. Other people are merely playing their part in fulfilling your karma (according to Döbereiner).

Dupuytren's Curvature (Contraction of the Hand Sinews)
Disease discloses the truth about ourselves as is here plain to see. Since your hand is being closed by force, you are obviously lacking in *openness*. There is also much aggression and hostility that you would like to conceal, but your *clenched* fist is revealing the true state of affairs. Become more open in spirit, and express your emotions more freely. This way you will gradually be able to receive again with *open hands*.

Fractures (broken bones in general)
Our bones symbolize stability and support as well as fulfillment of norms, and a bone fracture indicates that you have overlooked the end of a phase in your development. Now your body is forced to tell you to *break* with the past. It is also possible that you have been laying too much stress on physical activity and not enough on spirituality. Allow yourself to be interrupted in your course, or, better still, take a break yourself in what was maybe too rigid a course. If you are flexible in spirit, you will be flexible in the way you live. Be *pliant,* then your bones will *give in,* too, and won't need to break.

Foot Problems (in general)
Foot problems can be interpreted in a similar way as leg ones. (If the toes are affected, this will probably have to do with minor aspects of the future.) Here, too, there is a certain fear of the future, caused by a lack of understanding of the laws of life. By preventing you from *going forward* without difficulty, your foot problem is drawing your attention to this fear. Often there will also be too strong a will to *make progress,* and having foot problems will *slow you down.* Realize that progress consists of two poles — namely, those of rest and activity. Follow the message of your body and learn to rest when necessary. Find the peace inside yourself which is the source of truth and understanding, love and strength. Then you will be able to *make your way* through life again.

Gout

If you suffer from gout, your body is *rigid* and *stiff,* and your attitude to life has apparently been *inflexible* and *rigid* for a long time. Anger and impatience have deposited themselves in your thoughts and now you are forced to be inactive and quiet. It may well be that you wanted to dominate others with your autocratic behavior. Now you yourself are being dominated — namely, by your gout. Make a conscious attempt to find peace and tranquillity. Cultivate innner openness and receptivity and let others go their own way. Every one has a right to freedom, and if we can accept that everything is all right; it will be. Reiki will be a great help to you in this process.

Hip Problems (in general, including coxarthropathy, for example)

Hip problems also demonstrate a certain amount of rigidity and inflexibility. This is the result of fear of the future and your inability to come to decisions about important matters. Don't force yourself to make *progress.* Reiki will help you to develop tranquillity, vitality and trust, a good basis for making decisions and *advancing* in life. Every step made in this way will be genuine progress.

Sciatica (Lumbago)

Sciatic complaints prevent activity and force you to take more rest. Apparently you are overburdened and, in many cases, this complaint involves a certain fear of the future as well as financial worries. In many cases, people suffering with lumbago try to compensate for a feeling of inferiority by undertaking great deeds. Here, too, you should heed the call to rest. Be sure to do so consciously, and you will achieve inner tranquillity. Reiki will be a great help to you in this process. Accept and observe your fears and limitations without repressing them or taking any kind of compensatory action. Accept yourself and life without passing judgements. Then you will discover that good is everywhere and you will have the feeling that you are being given support and protection. Be joyful and optimisitic.

Knee Problems (in general)
If pride, stubborness, egotism or unconscious fears prevent you from *submitting* and *yielding* at times, this might result in *stiff* and *inflexible* knees. If you can succeed in developing more tolerance and sympathy and learn how to forgive, you will be able to forego the possibility of getting even worse knee problems in the future. Reiki is a truly wonderful method for such complaints. Once you have learned humility again, you will find it easier to *flex* your knees.

Paralysis (in general)
Paralysis is always a form of evading responsibility and is often caused by fear or shock. In many cases, the individual is mentally inflexible but will not admit to being so or represses the fact. Realize that you are part of all life and welcome all new experiences and changes that life bestows on you.

Hernia (a similar interpretation is valid for umbilical hernia)
Over-exertion, pressure, mental stress as well as a tendency towards self-punishment are at work here, and your creative energy has taken the wrong course. It is time you became aware of this and began to flow harmoniously with the current of your life in love and sensitivity. Accept yourself as you are. Give yourself love and Reiki.

Bechterew's Disease (Ancylosing spondylitis)
This disease is a manifestation of an unconscious inflexibility which is the result of an excessively strong ego. The individual is now being forced to see how rigid and inflexible he really is. Is it not better to practice humility than to be humiliated in such a manner? Learn to see beyond yourself and your own needs. Become more flexible, then you will be able to *walk upright* through life, full of joy and at peace with yourself and the world.

Multiple Sclerosis (MS)
Multiple sclerosis is often caused by the attempt to always have everything under control. Now your body is refusing to play along with this and is trying to tell you to let go of your *inflexibility* and your *iron will*. You have probably grown *hard in heart* and spirit. It is time you learn to flow joyously with the river of life. Stop trying to control and dominate everything. Relax

and let go completely. Have trust in your inner guidance, and give yourself Reiki as often as possible. Learning a method of relaxation or meditatation will also be of great help.

Muscular Cramps (in general)
A cramp is always the result of strong tension and indicates the wish to *hold on* to something. The things which the individual is not able to let go of are often long outlived and should have been buried and forgotten a long time ago. Now your energy is blocked and the cramps are an outlet for what has been repressed. It would be better for you to learn to leave the past behind. Relax, free yourself, and allow your life to flow in harmony. Learning a form of meditation might also be of great help, for, just like Reiki, it will teach you to *let go.*

Neck Complaints (as in stiffness of the neck for example)
Our neck has to do with obstinacy and stubborness, as the expression that someone is *stiff-necked* proves. Persons with neck complaints often refuse to regard a matter from different points of view and are usually unaware of their selfishness, rigidity and stubborness. If you learn to become more flexible and tolerant and to accept other people's opinions, your neck will not have to become so stiff. (Please see the Bible, Proverbs 29:1 and Nehemiah 9:16 in this respect.)

Polyarthritis
People suffering from polyarthritis are often compulsively fastidious and overly moralistic, frequently the result of inner *rigidity* and *obstinacy.* In most cases there is also a tendency to self-sacrifice, frequently caused by repressed aggressions which the individual is unwilling to admit to, because "everyone should see how much I have to struggle!" Although sacrifice is basically something very positive, you should take a critical look at your motives. Do they really have anything to do with genuine love. Do you grant others freedom and allow them to lead their own lives. If not, you should allow your consciousness the freedom it needs to develop and not restrict it with compulsive patterns of thought. Love, forgiveness, freedom and affirmation are values which are of particular importance in your case. Open yourself up to them.

Rickets
Emotions probably play a minor role in the lives of children who have rickets. If these symptoms also occur in old age, this might have been the case during adulthood too. If you are now suffering from rickets, there is probably not enough love and security in your life and you, therefore, lack a feeling of *inner stability*. One could even say that you are emotionally *undernourished*. Pay more attention to these aspects of life and remember that we are being continuously nourished and protected by the energies and love of the universe. In order to receive the warming rays of the sun, a flower merely needs to open its petals. Reiki works like this too. Open yourself up!

Rheumatism (in general)
Your conscious attitude is lacking in genuine love and, therefore, feelings of resentment bitterness and vindictiveness have built up within you to such an extent that they are now turning on your body in the form of an inflammatory process. Why don't you admit to having these emotions and feelings of aggression? Why do you repress them so strongly? Take a good look at these traits and at your obstinacy, inflexibility and domineering attitude without condemnation. Have compassion with yourself (and others), and learn to accept and love yourself with all your emotions and feelings, both positive and negative. In this way you will be able to break the spell caused by your negativity and give your feelings free rein again. Make generous use of Reiki.

Back Complaints (in general)
Our back gives our body *support* and keeps it *erect* and *upright*. Therefore, the back stands for *support* and *rectitude*. Problems with your back show that you are overburdened and that you are probably not willing to admit to this. It is also likely that you have the feeling of not receiving enough *support*. Complaints affecting the upper section of the spine have to do with a lack of emotional support, which results in a lack of inner stability. At the same time, you are probably a person who tends to hold back love and affection. Complaints affecting the lower area of the back have to do with financial and material worries and with fear of the future with regard to money. The power which created the universe and supports it gave life to you, too, and will maintain and support you on all levels of existence. All you have to do is open yourself up to this possibility instead of always relying on your small and limited ego. Give love and trust to others, and, in accordance with the Law of Affinity, you will receive both in return.

Torticollis
Torticollis is an indication of insecurity. Apparently you are not willing to *face the truth,* and prefer to avoid *confrontations,* and now you are being forced to *turn the other way.* Here, again, symptoms do not lie. You must overcome your *one-sided* attitudes and look at the other side of things without fear. Everything ceases to be threatening once you learn to regard it with awareness and accept what you see. If you learn to take up this attitude, your neck will be able to move freely again.

Bursitis (Housemaid's knee)
Bursitis indicates that you have held back anger and aggressions for too long a period of time. Now you would really like to *bang your fist on the table* or even hit someone. Try to find a harmless way of giving vent to your anger; you will surely find some way of doing so. Don't hold back your feelings or condemn them or pass judgement, but just watch them consciously. They are a form of energy and power. If you learn to accept them, they will be transformed into positive energy and the power of love will flow freely within you again.

Writer's Cramp
This symptom shows quite clearly that you are over-ambitious and pretentious. Who are you trying to impress? A cramp is always an indication of *excessive tension* and an attempt to represent something or someone that you are not. Spend more time on just being, instead of doing or wanting to do, and life will become relaxed and easy again. You are *somebody,* even without your exaggerrated sense of ambition. (Please see under **Muscular Cramps.**)

Shoulder Complaints (in general)
You have quite literally *shouldered* too much, and this has become too *heavy a burden for you to carry.* Take a good look at what you have *taken on,* and see whether all of it is necessary. Become brave enough to cast some off and have some *of the weight taken off your shoulders.* If you do this, your body will no longer have to warn you in such an uncomfortable manner and life will become freer and less of a *burden.*

Numbness of the Limbs

Here too, this symptom is an expression of something which you have been carrying around with you unconsciously for a long time. You are living in a state of emotional impoverishment and are holding back love and compassion. In fact, your feelings are as numb as your limbs. It is time you reacted more spontaneously to life and opened yourself up to feelings of love, happiness and harmony. Reiki will be of great help in awakening your feelings for all aspects of life.

Sprains (in general)

Sometimes we are too forceful in the way we deal with others. If we are unaware of this, a sprain will draw our attention to this fact. Yet why should we keep trying to force our will onto others. Let people live their own lives. They will be much happier this way and you won't need to sprain your ankle or wrist again.

Fracture of a vertabra

Fractures of the vertebrae reflect *inflexibility* and a one-sided outlook on life. Your attitudes are too rigid and, as a result, *fate has bent you down.* This could have been prevented by a little more humility on your part. Now you have time to reflect on this and should come to realize that life is always in motion and full of change. Learn to live all the aspects of life, learn to flow with them and life will become a joy again.

Infections

Infections (in general)
Every infection stands for a conflict that has not been consciously lived through and solved. Either you have not been able to perceive this conflict, or you have avoided dealing with it, or you have simply refused to admit to it. Be honest with yourself.

In order to gain attention, the psychological energy you have been trying to avoid has attracted causative organisms (viruses, bacteria or toxins), which have invaded your body. Now your powers of resistance have been activated, and the conflict you were seeking to avoid is *raging* in you in the form of an inflammation. Compaints involved in such processes usually end in "itis," as is the case with neuritis, bronchitis, etc. An acute inflammation is always an urgent call to understand something, while an inflammatory process which has become chronic points to an unsolved conflict of long standing. You evidently lack the courage to make a clear *decision* about solving a problem. Apparently, you feel you would lose something or have to give something up in doing so. Thus, your energies are blocked and you have become stagnant, for all your energy is now concentrated on the *focal infection,* and your body feels tired. The part of the body in which an inflammation takes place indicates the psychological causes of your conflict. We must therefore become keen observers of pathological phenomena if we are to decipher the meaning of a given disease.

If you don't voluntarily take a necessary step in your development, conflicts will arise. Take a look at the possibilities the situation offers you for inner growth. Take on the challenges life offers in order to learn and grow consciously and voluntarily. And, remember, in the case of a chronic conflict, it is important to bring it to an end by making a clear decision. (The word *decide* originally meant to *cut down* or *away,* as is still noticeable in terms like taking *decisive* action.)

Bronchitis (Please see under **Respiratory System**)

Colds (in general)
A cold indicates that a stagnant conflict is beginning to *loosen up* and that

certain *blocked-up channels* are ready to flow again. A cold rids your body of toxins, and afterwards you usually feel as if you had made a few small steps on your path of development. Accept your wish to rest and spend as quiet a time as possible. Try to deal with your conflicts by observing and accepting them. If you can succeed in doing this, you will emerge from your cold both cleansed and strengthened.

Pneumonia (please see under **Respiratory System**)

Hepatitis (please see under **Digestion/Elimination**)

Fever (in general)
Fever indicates a state of excitement, of *burning anger* which has not been dealt with and which is now manifested on the physical level. Take a good look at what is making you so angry or excited. It is part of your life, and every conflict you experience has something to tell you. Learn to accept whatever is troubling you, just as you accept the pleasant sides of life. Then you will become whole and will begin to *radiate* genuine love.

Influenza (in general)
Influenza is either a sign of too much stress or of a crisis you would like to evade, although you are unwilling to admit this to yourself at the time. You are fed up and would like to just let everything take its own course. Accept your wish for rest, and allow yourself to gather new strength. Consciously accept the situation you are in, for whatever it is, it contains a chance for growth. (Please see under **Colds**, too.)

Allergies

Allergies (in general)
An allergy is an overreaction of the body's immune system to a substance which has been declared an "enemy," since it symbolizes an aspect of the individual which is fought against, rejected or repressed. Fighting a self-created enemy is always an act of aggression, an unconscious fight against an area of life we are afraid of and do not want to let into our lives. Resistance is the opposite of love, for love means acceptance and becoming one. The substance which triggers off the allergic reaction is a symbol of the area of life you are avoiding and unconsciously fighting.
If you are suffering from allergic symptoms, it is time you asked yourself what your symbolic enemy is trying to tell you. What aspects of life do you avoid and repress? Try to take a conscious look at the things you are unconsciously afraid of, and observe your resistance to them, as well as your fear and inner aggression. You will come to realize that nothing is good or bad unless you make it that way. (In this context, read the Bible passages to be found in Mathew 5:39 and 5:44.) Make peace with yourself and the world. Genuine healing of your allergies will only be possible if you succeed in consciously integrating the aspects you have been avoiding as if they were enemies. This is the path of love, the path of Reiki.

Antibiotics Allergy
The term antibiotic is made up of the words *anti* against and *bios* life. These are drugs which work against life. They also kill something within you. An antibiotics allergy is a healthy reaction and an indication that you should accept all aspects of life, even when they take on the forms of tension or conflict.

House Dust Allergy
This type of allergy indicates a fear of all things that you feel are *impure and dirty,* a fear which is often projected onto sexuality.

Hay Fever
This is an allergic reaction to *pollen,* which is a symbol of fertilization and reproduction. Hay fever reflects unconscious resistance, especially where sexuality is concerned. There will frquently be much unconscious *fear* of sexuality, too.

Allergy to Animals (in general)
Every animal stands for love, instinctual urges and sexuality.

Allergy to Dogs
This type of allergy reflects a repression of the aggressive component of sexuality.

Allergy to Cats
A cat symbolizes the more feminime aspects of sexuality and qualities such as gentleness and tenderness. If you are allergic to cats, you may have problems with these areas.

Allergy to Horses
Horses represent the instinctual side of sexuality. If you are allergic to horses, this may mean that you are afraid of your sexual instincts. Once again, physical dis-ease shows where the truth of the matter lies.

Childhood Illnesses

Childhood Illnesses (in general)

All childhood illnesses affecting the skin, such as *measles, mumps, chicken-pox* and *scarlet fever* herald a new phase of development in the life of a child. Here, something which is still unknown to the child and which can, therefore, not be dealt with without conflict becomes visible on the surface of the skin. When such diseases run their course, you will find that children are more mature afterwards. During the illness, tell your child that everything is all right. Tell him that *life is a journey* where *new things* are constantly being *discovered* and that every *treasure* we find inside ourselves helps us to grow a little more. Give your child special attention and a feeling of trust during his illness as well as plenty of Reiki.

Cancer

Cancer (in general)
Cancer is life no longer governed by order, the result of disharmony among the cells of the body. When a person has cancer, the individual cell no longer submits to the overall organization of the body but leads an independent life of its own, multiplying regardless of the effects this has on the rest of the body. The German psychologist Thorwald Dethlefsen, compares cancer pathology to our modern world, which is characterized by ruthless expansion and a predominant pursuit of self-centered interests. Whether in the area of politics, economy, religion or private life, most individuals pursue their own interests, trying to strengthen their own position in life in order to achieve further egoistic ideas and goals. In the course of this ruthless striving, they also exploit their fellow-men and nature alike, and regard the world as a huge host organism. In a similar manner, the cancer cells also regard the body as a host organism which they can ruthlessly exploit to achieve their own ends. The death of the body also means the death of the cancer cells, but they are as oblivious to this fact as is modern man, who does not realize that if he destroys nature he will destroy himself. The cancer cells lack awareness of the body as a greater, encompassing whole, and do not realize that it is only in cooperation with other cells that they will be able to continue to exist. Just as the cell is part of the body, we ourselves are part of a world-encompassing unity.
If you have cancer, ask yourself which area of life you have cut yourself off from as a whole. The area of the body affected and the psychological problem it symbolizes will help you find this out. Accept yourself, in all your strength and weakness, and accept everything that happens to you, both positive and negative, and integrate it into your consciousness. This way you will be able to open yourself up to life as a whole and begin to experience that wonderful state where everything else is part of yourself, and where everything lives and functions in harmony. A method of healing like Reiki, as well as any other method which helps expand consciousness, will be of great help in this respect.

Psychological Problems

Bed-wetting

During the night, a child who wets his bed is letting go of what he did not
dare to let go of during the day, namely pressure exerted by parents, school,
etc. In a sense, bed-wetting is related to crying, for both are forms of releasing tension. Relieve your child of untoward pressure and give him or her
more love and understanding.

Depression (in general)

Depression is a state of severe *oppression* in which the depressed person tor-
tures himself or herself with self-reproach and feelings of guilt. Outwardly-
directed aggression makes the person feel unconsciously guilty and, therefore, he directs it back onto himself instead. Depression is also a form of
refusing responsibility (which can culminate in *suicide*), but it is hopeless;
your feelings of guilt confront you with your responsibility again. Depression can also occur when it is time to enter a new phase of life, as for example
in the case of puerperal depression. Depression can also confront you with
an area of life you have not come to terms with, such as old age, death,
loneliness, loss, etc. Look at the aspect of life that is causing your depression. Feel your way into it. Everything that life brings contains a summons
and a challenge to integrate just this very thing. Reiki will be of great help
to you in all these cases.

Exhibitionism

If you feel an urge to exhibit yourself, you have apparently never had the
chance to express your sexuality freely. You regard sex as something *unclean,*
whether consciously or unconsciously, and now this area of your life is
claiming its rights, confronting you with what you never wanted to see.
Realize that sex is a beautiful and important part of life. Give increased Reiki
to the Heart and Sacral Chakras, and your sexuality will regain its original
expression of being again.

Mental Disease (Psychosis)

There are many different discoveries, research findings and opinions regarding the forces and mechanisms that play a role in mental disease. Mental illness is usually a retreat from a reality that the individual is either unable to cope with or which is experienced as being too difficult or not rewarding enough. As a result, the patient's consciousness becomes open to areas which were previously only accessible to the unconscious. These areas or forces now begin to determine the person's behaviour beyond his conscious control, with psychotics frequently living out what had been previously prevented by social conformity. Through the illness, the individual involved is forced to get to know the unconscious forces that control him in order to integrate them. Generally, Second Degree Reiki will be of help in treating the mentally ill. Use the symbol for increasing strength during every treatment, and make use of the mental method to increase the individual's power of integration and his consciousness of the inner self. Since the inner self can face and integrate all forces without being overwhelmed, it will not be affected by the mental condition of the patient. If the person is very restless, the absentee method will be equally successful. Balancing out the Chakras has proved very beneficial in this respect.

Congenital Alexia (Word Blindness)
For people suffering from word blindness, intense occupation with "preserved thoughts," which is what written words basically are, is not of utmost importance. Instead, they should open themselves up more to the intuitive and creative aspects of life which their symptoms are pointing them to. If this step can be taken consciously, there will no longer be a reason for you to be word blind, and the condition will disappear. If you are word blind, look at what this state is forcing you to do or what it is preventing you from doing. Adults can help children to reach this important insight.

Tiredness
Great tiredness shows that life in general, or the responsibility you have to carry, has become so excessive that all you want to do now is retreat into an unconscious state (of sleep). Allow yourself the rest you are yearning for, and do not force yourself to activity. Go within, instead, and gather new strength. By doing this, you will find that you will enjoy being active again. Give yourself a lot of Reiki. A simple, natural form of meditation will also be of great help.

Nail Biting
Among other things, nails can be used for scratching and defending ourselves. Nail biting often indicates fear of showing pent- up aggressions, which frequently occurs when parents exert too much pressure on children already lacking in confidence. A child who bites his nails is trying to boost his self-confidence. Allow your child the freedom to freely express all aspects of his character without guilt.

Nervousness (in general)
Nervousness indicates a lack of inner peace and tranquillity, which is the result of excessive haste, anxiety and the wish to do everything especially well. Learn to trust the flow of life, and remember that you are on a never-ending path to eternity, so there's no need to hurry.

Fainting
Fainting is a reflection of inner weakness and the fear of not being able to cope with something, but it can also indicate fear of losing power. Learn to follow the events in your life and go with the flow. Accept everything that approaches you. You will soon discover that you already possess the strength and the knowledge that you need to come to terms with life and all that it brings. (See also under **Circulatory Collapse**.)

Motion Sickness (car, air and seasickness)
When you travel, you leave familiar surroundings behind you without being able to perceive what the future holds, and there are many new impressions to digest. It is this unconscious clinging to your accustomed surroundings and fear of the new which makes you dizzy and nauseous. Moreover, sitting in a car, boat, airplane or train makes you aware of the fact that you are in a situation which you cannot easily escape from. *Flow* with the motion of the vehicle. Give up your resistance, accept what is happening and open yourself up to all the new impressions flowing in on you. You will soon discover that the world is very beautiful if you live with it and not against it.

Insomnia (and problems with falling asleep)
Falling asleep is an act of trust which demands the ability to let go of activity and control and open oneself up to the unknown. Each time you fall asleep,

you die a "minor death." Moreover, once asleep, things which were suppressed during the day rise up out of the unconscious during the night. People who have difficulty falling asleep will usually have difficulty in dying, too, for they are not willing or capable of letting go. End your day properly, and prepare yourself for the night. Do not think of the coming day, for it will take care of itself. Simply open yourself up to what is to come and get to know and integrate the "dark" side of life.

Sexual Abnormality (and perversion in general)
In all cases of sexual abnormality, the individual involved is confronted with those aspects of his being which he rejects and which he frequently bitterly fights against. The form his sexual abnormality takes shows him the quality he is lacking, whether masculinity, femininity, humility, dominance, etc. In a sense, these abnormalities make a person *whole* by letting him live out the qualities he is lacking. Integrate antagonistic poles within yourself to a state of unity, and do not be forced to do so by extreme behaviour. In this way, you will soon enjoy sexuality in a *whole*some manner.

Stuttering
Stuttering prevents a free flow of lingual expression and communication. It points to the fact that your thoughts, emotions and urges make you feel insecure, and that you are unconsciously trying to control any outward expression of this fact. Open yourself to your thoughts, emotions and wishes and accept them without condemning them in any way. This way, your self-confidence will increase and you will find it easier to open yourself up to others.

Addiction (in general)
Addiction always involves a search for fulfillment. In this case however, you are not able to achieve it with your own strength and so you turn to a substitute instead. In the case of misuse of alcohol (please see also under **Alcoholism**), hashish and marijuana, it is a problem-free world that you are in search of and have not found, and now, by taking these drugs, you hope to blunt the *hardness* of life. Addiction to amphetamines or cocaine, which stimulate the capacity for activity and productivity, usually indicate a search for success and the love and recognition that go with it. An excessive use of LSD, mescaline, magic mushrooms and heroin addiction reflect a search for *kicks* and expansion of consciousness. Whatever drug you are addicted to

or take too much of, it means that you have let yourself be satisfied by a substitute for your real goal. Apparently, the pathway there was too difficult or troublesome for you. Maybe it seemed impossible to tread, or you came to a standstill at the very beginning of your journey. Maybe you never even set out on it because of self-condemnation or a lack of self-confidence. "Ask, and it shall be given you; seek, and ye shall find; knock, and it shall be opened unto you," Matthew 7:7.

Try to find out what it is you are searching for. Then look for a path that will lead you to this goal, one that you can readily follow. There must be a path to lead you there, otherwise you would not have felt the longing. Reiki will definitely help you to regain the self-confidence and strength necessary to free yourself of needing a substitute goal, so that you can take up your interrupted journey again. As a rule, a long series of treatment will be necessary if lasting results are to be achieved. There are various meditation techniques which will help you experience whatever it was you were trying to find with the help of drugs. It is much more rewarding to achieve your goal "alone." Make a new start.

Alcoholism
An indiscriminate use of alcohol is often the result of trying to escape conflicts. You try to *wash down* whatever it is you find too hard to *chew* and *digest*. People who turn to drink often experience feelings of futility, inferiortiy and guilt, which are all made worse by dependence on alcohol. Learn to love yourself with all your shortcomings and weaknesses. Admitting to these aspects of yourself will be the first step in overcoming them. Apart from Reiki, meditation will help you to find peace, self-respect and well-being and give you the strength to solve your problems instead of evading them. (Please see under **Addiction**.)

Bulimia (excessive appetite)
Compulsive eating reflects a *hunger for life, love and emotional nourishment*. There is a feeling of *emptiness* inside you which you desparately try to *fill* up in a physcial way as you see no other way of overcoming it. Frequently, the individual involved is very insecure and afraid of loss. Learn to accept and love yourself as you are, then you will find it easier to open up the limitations of your ego and take in spiritual nourishment. At the same time, become aware of the fact that there is an inexhaustable source of love and fulfillment within you, if only you would find it and make use of it.

Anorexia Nervosa
This disturbance almost exclusively affects young girls during puberty. It symbolizes the unconscious wish to escape from the physical aspects of femininity and sexuality, and is manifested by a strong yearning for purity and self-abnegation. If you suffer from this complaint, try to accept the feminine side of yourself, try to accept that you have a yearning for warmth, intimacy and sexuality. Remember, it is only when you accept all areas of life that you will be able to attain inner wholeness and real freedom.

Excessive Desire for all that is sweet
If you have an undue craving for sweets, you are probably missing out on the *sweetness* of life, which in turn reflects an unappeased *hunger* for love. In children this condition frequently indicates that they do not feel loved enough. If you have an excessive desire for sweet things, give yourself the love and recognition you are yearning for and accept yourself as you are. Then you will be able to give love to others and a real exchange will come about. If your child is always nibbling and eating sweets, give it more love and attention. (Please see under **Bulimia**.)

Nicotine Addiction
The lungs symbolize the idea of freedom and communication (please see under **Respiratory System**), which you are trying to conjure up by smoking. However, your wishes become more and more *nebulous* in the process. Become aware of what you really want, then you will be able to live things out more easily. Genuine communication can only take place in an *atmosphere of clarity*. Have the courage to communicate with life whole-heartedly.

Compulsive Neurosis (in general)
Compulsive neurosis has to do with massive repression of an area of life which is regarded as being extremely negative. Your compulsive neurosis confronts you most strongly with the very aspect you are repressing in order to make you learn to accept this area of life. Once you are able to do so, you will no longer need the neurosis, for all it is trying to tell you is to accept and integrate whatever it is you have been avoiding. Take a square look at what you have been rejecting, and do so without passing judgement. If you manage to do this, your neurosis will not have to compensate for your one-sidedness and you will become healthy and whole again.

Miscellaneous

Complaints of old age (in general)
Complaints of old age point to problems and one-sided attitudes which were not solved or integrated during earlier years. Your symptoms symbolize the problems and attitudes involved, so take a good look at them. Once you have realized what these are, you can try to integrate them and accept them consciously. If you succeed in doing this, you are to be congratulated, for your specific complaints will disappear.

Congential Defects (in general)
Congenital defects point to unsolved problems from a past life. It was your own choice to be born into this life as you were, so do not try to put the blame on others. The defect involved symbolizes whatever it is you still have to learn. See your handicap as a chance for growth towards a greater wholeness.

Disturbances Caused by Geopathic Zones (such as crossing water veins)
If a geopathic zone is causing some kind of complaint, we should try to see what the symptoms it is causing are trying to tell us. Generally, this will be to *change* something in our lives. Of course, it will be necessary to work and sleep at another place in the home, but we also have to carry out some changes in our mental and spiritual attitudes, too, for it would seem that something one-sided has managed to creep inside us and is now making us ill.
Therefore, do not only change the position of your bed or desk, etc. (with the help of a dowser, if necessary) but take a good look at stubborn and one-sided parts of yourself, too. A *change of position* will work wonders.

Pain
Pain is always an interruption of the flow of life and is often the result of repressed feelings. The area of the body where you feel pain symbolizes some inner aspect of yourself where you feel fettered and unfree. Do not condemn or repress the pain — it has something important to tell you. Give it your full attention; go into it, feel it with all your consciousness, and tell

it that it is welcome. If you do this, the pain will have fulfilled its function and will disappear. In order to make sure it doesn't return, however, turn your attention to the psychological aspect of yourself it was symbolizing. This is the area in which you must let go of something; maybe even the wish for punishment. Let go, and you will learn to flow with life again.

Accidents

Each and every one of us bears the full responsibility for our lives and for everything we experience. Even accidents do not *happen* to us, but are brought about by ourselves, although this generally takes place unconsciously. When an accident happens to you, the course you are presently following is suddenly put into question. If you analyze how the accident happened, you will soon *hit* on the underlying problem. Could it be that you have *lost your grip* on things, or that they have made you *stumble* and *fall*? Are you losing *control*? Have you been *thrown off your course* in any way? Maybe you haven't been able to *stop in time* in some situation, or have *overlooked* something. Could it be that you were *half-asleep* when the accident happened, or have you been *meeting with great resistance* lately? Take a close look at how the accident happened, and pay attention to verbal hints — they will generally help you in your interpretation. Interesting statistical evaluations of accidents point clearly to the fact that some people are what is known as "accident personalities" — people who unconsciously try to solve their problems and conflicts by having accidents. Having found out the "inner" reason for an accident, work on it. In this way you will have some very interesting insights and be able to make good progress in growth and development.

Forgetfulness

If you keep forgetting things, this could be a sign that you should learn to forget something which you have been holding on to and not wanted to let go, such as some event of the past. If this is the case, it is probable that you have been turning your thoughts again and again to the same old problems without really solving anything. Try consciously letting go of these things; leave the past in peace and do not cling to the things of yesterday. *Be here now,* and open yourself up to the wonders of life with each day. If you can manage to really forget the things of the past, you won't need to be forgetful any more.

Whenever beauty is perceived, ugliness arises.
Whenever good is perceived, evil arises.
Existence gives rise to non-existence,
And confusion brings about simplicity.
High gives rise to low,
Noise brings about silence,
And before opposes after in sequence.
Therefore, the truly wise man goes about doing
nothing and teaching without words.
He possesses all and achieves unity with everything.
He produces, but he does not possess.
He rounds off his life but does not claim success.
Because he does not claim, he cannot lose.

Lao Tse

TAO TE CHING, verse 2nd

Chapter 27

The Story of this Book

Shalila would now like to tell you how this book came about.
"A few years ago, Bodo and I had a great longing for a time of fasting and meditation in pure, peaceful surroundings.
Some Austrian friends of ours found a four-hundred year old chalet situated about 4,300 feet up in a wonderful open valley in the Tirolean Alps of Austria, where we could go and stay for a while. Here we found all we had been looking for; namely, absolute peace and quiet, clean air and a spring of pure mountain water. At last we could begin to fast.
On the tenth day, Bodo began to suffer one of the crises that often happen during fasting. He was feeling weak and dizzy, and every kind of movement was too difficult for him. He wasn't even able to pull himself up to meditate that evening, but lay beside me, exhausted, instead.
It was time to give some of our faraway patients absentee treatment and, having done so, it occurred to me that I could treat Bodo this way, too, which I then did for 20 minutes without his knowledge. Just after I had finished, Bodo suddenly opened his eyes and said, "Just imagine, I've been thinking about Reiki all the time, and I think it's time to write a book about it." He then went on to tell me how he would divide the book up, the chapters he would include, and so on.
The next day he could hardly wait to get up and sit down at the old oak table and start writing his book. All the problems of the previous day had disappeared, and he was full of energy and activity again.
I was busy translating "Maharishi at 433" at the time, but Bodo's enthusiasm was so infectious I began working on the Reiki book with him. We soon ran out of paper, and the next village was twenty kilometres away, down in the valley. Luckily, a friend of ours made the long and dangerous journey to our chalet and happened to have in his car a large packet of information material printed on only one side in his car, and so we were able to continue working on the book.
We wrote much of this book in a blossoming alpine meadow under the hot

summer sun, and when things got too hot for us, we would go off and bathe in the icy mountain stream. On rainy days, work was continued indoors in the chalet.

Our time of fasting sped by in no time at all, and Bodo got ideas so quickly he could hardly set them down onto paper. Being a more deliberate and cautious kind of person myself, it was my task to go over his ideas and work them over in detail, and so we made a good team. When the time came to take our leave of the mountains, the first hand-written version of this book was already finished. Back home on the island of Sylt, a few more details were added and worked over and, before long, we had even found the right person to do the illustrations."

We very much hope that the words and thoughts concerning the Reiki art of healing which are contained in this book will accompany you on part of your way.

Follow the events of life,
for they will lead you to people
and places
which will further your inner growth.

Phyllis Lee Furumoto

Contact address of the authors of this book (in case of criticism or ideas):
Bodo J. Baginski and Shalila Sharamon
"Song of Nature", Vale Cove, Ardnatrush, Glengarriff, Co. Cork, Ireland.

We, the authors are not connected with, nor do we represent, any specific
Reiki Group. We see ourselves as facilitators for the Universal Life Energy.
Please check your local community resource magazine for Reiki practitioners
or write for more information to these organizations— there are many others.

The Reiki Alliance   Traditional Reiki Network
P.O. Box 41   Fire No. 602 Case Hill Road
Cataldo ID 83810   Treadwell NY 13846-0262
208/682-3535   Tel. & Fax: (607) 829-3702
                                            or
The Center for Reiki Training   27, Bethlehem Road
 29209 Northwestern Hwy #592   93553 Jerusalem
Southfield MI 48034   Israel
Tel: (313) 948-8112   Tel: 972-2-671-4964

Bodhidharma Sch. of Reiki Healing Reiki Center for Healing Arts
P.O. Box 773   San Mateo CA (415) 345-7666
Avila Beach CA 93424

Please Note:
A Reiki Master does not have to belong to any of these organizations, but
generally does so.

REIKI OUTREACH INTERNATIONAL
Reach Outreach International came into being on June 21, 1990 for the purpose
of creating a world-wide network of Reiki practitioners who are united in service
to humanity and planet Earth. The vision of Reiki Outreach International is for
thousands of Reiki practitioners to direct the healing power of Reiki daily, or as
often as possible, to specific world situations and crises. The exact form of the
transmissions is communicated to participants through a world-wide network of
telephone contacts which are available 24 hours a day. This united energy is a
major contribution to world peace and harmony.
World Headquarters: Mary A. McFadyen, Founder, R.O.I., P.O. Box 609,
Fair Oaks CA 95628, USA. Telephone: (916) 863-1500, Fax: (916) 863-6464.
European Center: Jürgen Dotter, European Coordintor, R.O.I., P.O. Box 326,
D-83090 Bad Endorf, Germany. Telephone/Fax: 08053-9242.

....Books are only of value
When they lead us toward life
And serve and benefit the living.
Every hour spent reading
Is wasted
If the reader does not experience
A spark of energy,
A presentiment of rejuvenation,
An idea of new life.

Herman Hesse

A COMPLETE BOOK OF
REIKI HEALING

Heal Yourself, Others, and the World Around You

by Brigitte Müller & Horst Günther

A Complete Book of

REIKI

HEALING

Brigitte Müller • Horst H. Günther

LIFERHYTHM

192 pages, 70 photographs
$15.95

This book is a complete illustrated guide to Reiki healing. It gives a history of Reiki and information about how to become a Reiki channel. It shows all the Reiki hand positions and gives suggestions for treating specific ailments. There are instructions for treating plants and animals and diagrams of the physical bodies of cats, dogs, and horses. Also included are sections on giving Reiki to expectant mothers, on giving first aid, and on caring for the dying patient.

✳✳✳

Brigitte Müller was the first Reiki Master in Europe. She gave herself to a life of Reiki healing and writes of her own experiences with the freshness of discovery. Horst Günther's life was transformed by Reiki also, after a serious accident left him for weeks in a hospital. Together they tell their inspirational stories.

LIVING REIKI: TAKATA'S TEACHINGS

Stories from the Life of Hawayo Takata
as told to
Fran Brown

In this loving memoir to her teacher, Fran Brown has gathered the colorful stories told by Hawayo Takata during her thirty-five years as the only Reiki Master teaching. The stories create an inspirational panorama of Takata's teachings, filled with the practical and spiritual aspects of a life given to healing.

Reiki is the energy of life. In the Usui System of Natural Healing, this energy is honored and used as a guide in daily life. It offers a simple path to perceive and experience our lives as a sacred honorable experience. These stories are illustrations from the life of a woman who lived the Reiki teachings. They are funny and serious, happy and sad, representing her own Japanese/Hawaiian upbringing and always demonstrating her deep trust in the Life Energy. The stories also show the growth of Takata's healing power and the simplicity with which she accepted it. From humble beginnings she became a great figure of strength, loved and respected by all who knew her.

$12.95

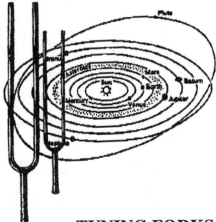

John C. Pierrakos M.D.

C ● R E
ENERGETICS

Developing the Capacity to Love and Heal

LifeRhythm
PUBLICATIONS

$18.95
300 pages
with 16 pages
of 4-color illustrations
of auras and chakras
ISBN: 0-940795-08-6

CORE ENERGETICS by John C. Pierrakos, M.D.
Developing the Capacity to Love and Heal

The therapeutic work of John C. Pierrakos, M.D. is based on these principles: 1. The person is a psychosomatic unity; 2. The source of healing lies within the self; 3. All of existence forms a unity that moves toward creative evolution, both of the whole and of the countless components.

Dr. Pierrakos developed his concept of Core Energetic Therapy, of power of the human center, by combining basic Reichian therapy with insights of modern physics as well as his own physical, mental and spiritual experiences and the inspirational lectures channeled by Eva Pierrakos which evolved into the Pathwork.

In this book, the pulsation of life does not remain a philosophical structure. Dr. Pierrakos clarifies for us what can be seen of human energy centers (chakras) and the various energy fields (auras). By relating the pulsation frequencies and colors of the fields of human beings, animals, plants and minerals, he defines the state of health or dysfunction. Through his experience as a practicing psychiatrist, body-therapist and his work in the laboratory, Dr. Pierrakos has developed a system for evaluating the state of the organism in terms of illness and health.

John Pierrakos's work, Core Energetics, *is necessary study for all those who do hands-on body work. Core energetics unifies all human aspects of physical, emotional, rational and spiritual into a powerful system to understand ourselves. I have great respect for Dr. Pierrakos: his work and his life speak for themselves.*
Barbara Brennan, Ph.D.

John Pierrakos, M.D.has written a provocative explanation of living forms and how they are interconnected. He sees the bodily microcosm and presents a lucid, speculative model of the interface between these realms. One finishes reading this book filled with wonder, and determined to accept the responsibility assigned by Pierrakos in order to transform oneself and one's world.
Stanley Krippner, Ph.D. Saybrook Institute

For Information about Core Energetics contact:
Core Energetic Evolution
PO Box 806, Mendocino CA 95460
Tel: (707) YES-CORE or (707) 937-1825 Fax: (707) 937-3052

LifeRhythm Publications

Ron Kurtz BODY-CENTERED PSYCHOTHERAPY:
THE HAKOMI METHOD
The Integrated Use of Mindfulness, Nonviolence and the Body
212 pages, illustrations
Some of the origins of Hakomi stem from Buddhism and Taoism, especially concepts like gentleness, compassion, mindfulness, and going with the grain. Other influences come from general systems theory, which incorporates the idea of respect for the wisdom of each individual as a living organic system that spontaneously organizes matter and energy and selects from the environment what it needs in a way that maintains its goals, programs and identity. Hakomi is a synthesis of philosophies, techniques and approaches that has its own unique artistry, form and organic process.

Helmut G. Sieczka CHAKRA BREATHING
A Pathway to Energy and Harmony
100 pages Illustrations Supplemental Cassette Tape of Guided Meditations
A guide to self-healing, this book is meant to help activate and harmonize the energy centers of the subtle body. Through the practice of chakra breathing we can learn to explore and recognize our innate possibilities, uncovering hidden energy potentials. The breath is the bridge between body and soul. In today's world as our lives are determined by stressful careers and peak performance, the silent and meditative moments have become more vital. We can try to remember our true selves more often, so that our natural energy balances can be restored. Chakra-breathing enhances this kind of awareness and transformational work, especially on the emotional and energetic level.

R. Stamboliev THE ENERGETICS OF VOICE DIALOGUE
Exploring the Energetics of Transformational Psychology
100 pages
Voice Dialogue is a therapeutic technique based on the transformational model of consciousness. This book approaches the human psyche as a synthesis of experience-patterns which may be modified only when the original pattern of an experience has been touched, understood and felt from an adult, integrated perspective, developing an "Aware Ego". This book explores the energetic aspects of the relationship between client and therapist, offering exercises for developing energetic skills and giving case histories to illustrate these skills. This book is a unique expression of the work of Hal and Sidra Stone Ph.Ds, creators of Voice Dialogue. Voice Dialogue is taught in the USA and now in many parts of the world.

R.Flatischler THE FORGOTTEN POWER OF RHYTHM
TA KE TI NA
160 pages, illustrations *Supplemental CD or Cassette*
Rhythm is the central power of our lives; it connects us all. There is a powerful source of rhythmic knowledge in every human being, and as we find our way back to this ancient wisdom, we unite with the essence of our life. Reinhard Flatischler presents his brilliant approach to rhythm is this book, for both the layman and the professional musician. TA KE TI NA offers an experience of the interaction of pulse, breath, voice, walking and clapping which awakens our inherent rhythm in the most direct way—through the body. It provides a first hand knowledge of the rhythmic roots of all cultures and a new understanding of the many musical voices of our world.

Malcolm Brown, Ph.D. THE HEALING TOUCH
An Introduction to Organismic Psychotherapy
320 pages 38 illustrations
A moving and meticulous account of Malcolm Brown's journey from Rogerian-style verbal psychotherapist to gifted body psychotherapist. Dr. Brown developed his own art and science of body psychotherapy with the purpose of re-activating the natural mental/spiritual polarities of the embodied soul and transcendental psyche. Using powerful case histories as examples, Brown describes in theory and practice the development of his work; the techniques to awaken the energy flow and its integration with the main Being centers: Eros, Logos, the Spritual Warrior and the Hara.

John C. Pierrakos M.D. EROS, LOVE & SEXUALITY
The Forces That Unify Man and Woman
128 pages

The free flow of the three great forces of life—eros, love and sexuality—is our greatest source of pleasure. These three forces are different aspects of the life force, and when we stay open they are experienced as one. They generate all activity, all creativity. This book has been long awaited. John Pierrakos, the great psychiatrist, was a student and colleague of Wilhelm Reich, and co-founder of Bioenergetics; he later developed his own therapeutic work, Core Energetics, which integrates the higher dimensions into our physical existence.

Allan Sachs D.C. The Authoritative Guide to
GRAPEFRUIT SEED EXTRACT
A Breakthrough in Alternative Treatment for Colds, Infections, Candida,
Allergies, Herpes, Parasites and Many Other Ailments *128 pages*
Dr. Allan Sachs' innovative work in treating Candida albicans imbalance, food allergies and environmental illness has inspired thousands of patients and a generation of like-minded physicians. Based on his training as a medical reseracher at New York's Downstate Medical Center and his intense interest in plants, he undertook a serious study of the antimicrobial aspects of certain plant derivatives, especially grapefruit seeds. This complete handbook gives all information on the therapeutic use of grapefruit seeds and also details their use for many household, farming and industrial needs and animal treatments.

LIFE RHYTHM

Connects you with your Core and entire being — guided by Science, Intuition and Love.

We provide the tools for growth, therapy, holistic health and higher education through publications, seminars and workshops.

If you are interested in our forthcoming projects and want to be on our mailing list, send your address to:

LIFERHYTHM   P.O. Box 806,   Mendocino, CA 95460 USA
Tel: 707/937-1825   Fax: 707/937-3052